The Awakened Woman
A Sacred Guide to Self-Mastery

Dedication

To the women who found their way here —
the ones quietly questioning,
the ones slowly unraveling,
the ones who've carried too much for too long.
To the ones who are tired of pretending.
Who crave honesty, softness,
and the safety to be fully seen.
This is for you.

And to the girl I'm raising —
my daughter,
the woman you are becoming.

May you never have to unlearn what I had to survive.
May your power feel like peace.
May your softness never be a sacrifice.

This is for every one of you.
This is for the ones who came before me.
And this is for every sacred *"yes"* that brought us here.

— *Tacara*

Published by House of Her Publishing
Fort Myers, Florida

ISBN: 979-8-218-65144-2

Printed in the United States of America
First Edition

Table of Contents

How to Use This Guide

Before we begin, let me say this—
Don't just write about what happened.
Write about how it made you feel.
This isn't just about remembering experiences.
It's about telling the truth about how those experiences
shaped you.

And stop overexplaining it.

No more "but other people had it worse."
No more "I'm just dramatic."
No more "I know I should be grateful..."

Feel that shit.

You don't need to justify your pain.
You don't need to excuse your anger.
You don't need to minimize your ache.

You're here to heal.

And I'll be right here with you, guiding you through this process—
if you'll let me.

At the end of each chapter, you'll find a lined journal page for
your reflections.
You're encouraged to use that space to answer the following
questions.
But if your truth needs more space—
if what you're carrying feels too big for one page—
grab a separate journal and keep going.
Activations and rituals can be revisited.
You are not meant to complete them just once.
If a particular one stirs something in you, return to it.
If you feel nothing the first time, do it again.

The Moment I Woke Up *(Prologue)*

There was a single moment that changed everything.
I didn't know it then, but that moment was the catalyst—
the breaking point.
The last time I would ever allow myself to be trapped in a life
that was not meant for me.
It was the last day my child's father was in our home.
We had been fighting again.
But this time, something was different—
I was different.
I wasn't just tired. I was soul tired.
I had been trying so hard.
Trying to understand him.
Fix things.
Make sense of his behavior, his moods, his silence.
He had been giving me the silent treatment for days—
withholding his presence like a punishment.
And I was just... so fucking tired.
Then suddenly, he spoke. His energy shifted.
His whole demeanor changed.
He came to me with a proposal—
he was going back over the road as a truck driver.

*"I talked to my mom about it, and she said I need to do whatever I
have to do for my family."*

And that was when it hit me.
He didn't see me as his family.
He made a decision that directly affected our home, our daughter,
our life—without me.
And he never even asked me.
And the way he presented it?

Like he was doing me a favor, like he was some great man
making a sacrifice for the greater good.
I felt it—the shift.
The lightness in his energy. The fucking relief in his voice.
And I realized right then—
I was never his home.
I was never his peace.

I was his prison.

The weight of that truth sank into my bones.
And suddenly, I wasn't tired anymore.
I was awake.
He told me that taking this job meant canceling my birthday
cruise—a trip that was already paid for.
And then a fire rose inside me.
He was making this decision for himself, disguising it as a
sacrifice for "his family," and expected me to accept it.
I called my mother, breathless with anger, exhaustion, and a
realization.

"I can't take this anymore. I'm so tired."

He made this life-changing decision without me.
That moment was the beginning of the end.
And the next day, I couldn't hold it in anymore.

I *crashed out.*
I let go.
I didn't give a fuck about keeping the peace.

I wasn't going to be silent anymore.
I wasn't going to swallow my feelings.
I wasn't going to make myself small so that he could be
comfortable.

And we haven't seen him since.

Maybe he changed his number. Maybe he ran.
Maybe disappearing was easier than facing me.
Maybe it was never about the job.
Maybe he was just looking for a way out.
A clean exit.
A final punishment for a woman who finally stopped begging to
be chosen.
But I do know this:
That was the moment I chose me.
That was the moment I woke up.

And that was the moment everything changed.

A Message to the Woman Who Feels Stuck

If you are in a cycle breaking you, listen to me—
you are not stuck.
You are not bound to him, or whoever in your life is draining you,
family included.
You don't need anyone's permission to reclaim yourself.
Your healing is on the other side of the door you haven't walked
through yet.

But you have to make a decision.

You have to get so sick of your shit that you refuse to stay in it
another second.
It's not about anyone else anymore.
It's about *you*.
Will you choose yourself?

Mantra: *"I am no longer available for anything that does not honor me."*

This book is a map—a guide.
A sacred initiation into the woman you were always meant to be.
But before we go any further, I need you to know—
this isn't a book you rush through.
There will be moments that ask you to pause and reflect, and to feel what's rising instead of skipping past it.
Give your spirit as much time as it needs.
There is no final destination here.

Healing is like a cycle—
sometimes it might feel like you're moving in circles, but each time you return, you're discovering more about who you are.
In this process, you'll peel back layers—
the layers of accumulated experiences, of the moments that shaped you, of the things you've carried silently.
These layers aren't just memories or stories—
they are parts of you that are waiting to be understood, waiting to be felt, to be seen for what they truly are.
And with every layer you uncover, you heal just a little bit more.

Healing isn't about having everything figured out.
It's not about rushing to the finish line, hoping to arrive at some perfect version of yourself.
Healing requires patience.
And the most important thing you can give yourself in this process is time.
It's about showing up for yourself, moment after moment, with curiosity, with honesty, and with grace—
even when it's hard to be kind to yourself.
This journey is about going beyond the surface.

It's about feeling it all—
the messiness, the discomfort, the fear and letting it shape you.
This is the kind of work that calls for radical truth, where you sit
with yourself in your rawest form and embrace *everything* you are.

And that's why we get real here.

But don't run from it.
There may be moments where you feel the rage I felt when I first
began to wake up.
You may feel sad.
You may grieve.

Allow it.

If you need to scream, if you need to cry—
give yourself full permission to do that now.
Because this is the safest space you've ever had to feel it.
And the truth is that you don't have to be fully healed to begin.
You just have to be *willing*.
Willing to see.
Willing to feel.
Willing to remember who you are.

Chapter 1: The Awakening

Put this book down if you're not ready.

I'm serious.
If you're here for another feel-good self-help read, this isn't that.
This book is not here to coddle you.
It's not here to make you comfortable.
It's here to rip the blinders off, to shake you out of your bullshit,
and to remind you of the power you've been handing away for far
too long.
Because the truth is, you've been asleep.
You've been conditioned—programmed, to be small.
You've been taught to make digestible yourself just to make others
comfortable.
To say yes when your body was screaming no.
To tolerate things that should've never even been options.

And now? Now you're feeling it.
That pressure in your chest.
That subtle knowing in the pit of your stomach.
The voice inside you is getting louder, telling you *this ain't it*—
that you were never meant to live in survival mode.
You were never meant to be chosen last—
not by love, not opportunity, and, sure as hell, not by yourself.

This is an awakening.

And once you see the truth, you can't unsee it.
Once you wake up to who you truly are, how you move, how you
think, how you exist in this world will never be the same.
This process will demand shit from you.
It will require you to stop making excuses.
To stop hiding behind your past.

To stop tolerating people, habits, relationships that are draining
the life out of you.
And once you step into your full power?
Everything shifts.
You no longer settle for less than you deserve.
You no longer accept anything that doesn't align with your
essence.
You no longer tolerate what disrupts your peace.

You attract what's meant for you.
You move with intention.
You command every damn room you step into.

But here's the thing:
This is not a smooth ride.
There will be days where you feel fucked up.
Where you doubt yourself, question everything, and feel like it's
all too much.
But trust me when I say this:
The work is worth it.
The discomfort is part of the process.
The struggle? It's the part of you that needs to fall away.

This book is your initiation into that version of yourself.

And let me tell you—
that "calm" you were clinging to?
It was killing you.
That version of peace you learned to perform?
It was just silence dressed up as safety.
And this fire rising in you now?
It's not chaos.
It's your return.

So I'll say it one last time.

If you're not ready, put this book down.

Close it and walk away.

But if you are ready, if you can feel that fire building inside you—
grab a pen and turn the page.

Chapter 2: Breaking Generational Cycles

This is for the woman who's tired of pretending she's okay.
Tired of holding it all together.
Tired of being strong for everybody but herself.
The woman who's been the healer, the backbone, the go-to—
but deep down, she wonders:
Who's ever really shown up for me?
This is for the woman who's been overlooked, underestimated,
and still showed up with love.
The one who learned to protect herself by staying quiet, playing
small, or giving too much.
The one who carried everyone else, and left herself behind.

But not anymore.

This is for the woman who's ready to remember who the hell she
is.
The one who's ready to feel again, to release, and to rise.
To meet herself in the mirror and finally say:
I got you.
Not just in survival—
but in softness, truth, and wholeness.
This is for the woman who's done abandoning herself, dimming
her light, and waiting to be chosen.
She's choosing herself now.
And this?
This is the beginning of everything.
And if that's you—
welcome home.

The Stories You Were Given

Let's talk about where it all began—
Not just what you've been through, but what you were taught to believe was normal.
We inherit patterns, beliefs, and wounds before we even understand what they mean.
We are shaped by the words our mothers spoke over us—
and the ones they didn't.
By the unhealed pain passed down through generations and the unspoken expectations of what it means to be a woman.
Some of us were raised to be small. To be quiet. To be self-sacrificing.
Some of us were raised to believe that survival is struggle.
That love must be earned and we are only as valuable as what we can provide.
But none of that is ours.
Breaking generational cycles is not just about recognizing the trauma of our lineage.
It is about choosing something different.
It is about deciding that we are no longer carrying what was never meant for us.

Reflection
What story have you inherited about who you are supposed to be?
Does it serve you?

Call It Out: The Shit You Were Taught Isn't Sacred

Let's stop playing nice with the things that are breaking us.

You don't have to drink your pain into silence because that's what you saw growing up.

You don't have to tolerate men who cheat, disrespect you,
and then come lay up like they didn't just humiliate you.
You don't have to keep handing out second, third, twentieth
chances just because your mama said, "he's still your daddy."
You don't have to smile through disrespect.
You don't have to be the strong one all the damn time.
You don't have to keep showing up for people who never show up
for you.
That's not loyalty —
it's self-abandonment dressed up as tradition.
You don't have to carry trauma like a family heirloom.
You don't have to keep cooking the same heavy-ass food that
clogs your arteries and emotions.
You don't have to clean your plate or keep your mouth shut
to keep the peace.

And let's talk about therapy for a second.

Black folks, especially —
we have been taught to suffer in silence.
To pray it away, to mind our business, and to keep family secrets
locked in the basement like they're not molding the walls of our
mind.
That's not healing, it's hiding.
You're not crazy for wanting help.
You're not weak for wanting peace.
You're not broken for wanting something different.

You are breaking the cycle.
And breaking a cycle doesn't mean you hate your family —
it means you love yourself enough to do better.
It means you're brave enough to say:
I'm not doing this shit anymore.

You get to stop.
You get to rest.
You get to love differently.
You get to eat, to parent, and to *live* differently.
You get to be free.

If nobody's said it to you before, let me say it:
It is safe to be different.
It is sacred to choose healing.
It is powerful to choose yourself.

This ends with you.

The Choice to Rebuild

Healing is not just about letting go—
it is about reclaiming.
When you decide to break a cycle, you are not just healing for
yourself—
you are healing for the women who came before you and the
women who will come after you.
You are rewriting your lineage in real-time.

Mantra: *I honor my ancestors by choosing my own path.*

We are more than our inherited stories.
We are more than the wounds passed down to us.
We are more than the silent burdens we were taught to carry.

When I became a mother, I realized—
I had the power to stop the cycles that tried to pass through me.
My daughter would not inherit what I had the courage to face and
refuse to pass down.

She will know she can be deeply in tune with her emotions—
and still be strong.
She will know she is more than what she does for others.
And she will never have to unlearn what I had to unlearn.
Because I choose healing, she will know freedom.

Being the first in your lineage to break cycles is not easy.
You will feel resistance, question yourself, and grieve the version
of you that once believed in the stories you were given.
You may feel alone.
But you are not.
Your ancestors are watching.
Your future children are waiting.
Your healed self is already standing in the future, calling you
forward.

Ancestral Healing in Action

Close your eyes and imagine the women who came before you
standing behind you.
Imagine their hands on your shoulders and eyes filled with love.
Some of them never got the chance to heal.
But you?
You are their answered prayer.
When you heal, you heal backward and forward in time.
When you choose love, peace, and alignment—
your lineage shifts.
You become the bridge between the pain of the past and the
freedom of the future.

Activation

1. Reflect on what cycles you refuse to pass down.
2. Speak aloud: "It ends with me."
3. Write the story you were always meant to live
- What does your healed lineage look like?
- How does your future self move through the world?
- Who do you become when you are no longer carrying what was never yours?

Closing Ritual

Sometimes, breaking cycles requires a symbolic release.
Try this ritual to cut energetic ties to generational wounds.
Close your eyes. Take a deep breath.
Envision a cord connecting you to the patterns, beliefs, or wounds you wish to release.
With love, tell it:

You have served your time. You do not belong to me.
I release you with gratitude, not resentment.
You were the survival, but I am the healing.

Now, imagine cutting the cord and watching it dissolve into light.
Breathe into the space where it once was—
filling it with new intention, new energy, new freedom.

Shadow Work Integration

If breaking generational cycles were easy, everyone would do it.

But let's be honest—
this isn't just about healing.
This is about confronting the weight of expectation, guilt, and obligation.

If you feel resistance around letting go of inherited trauma, ask yourself:
- Who taught me that suffering equals worth?
- Why do I feel guilty for choosing a different path?
- Have I been conditioned to believe that breaking free is selfish?

This is where your work begins.
If you feel discomfort, do not look away—
question it.

Final Words

You were chosen to break the cycle for a reason.
Not because you were the strongest—
but because you were the most *willing*.
The work is not easy.
The pain is not imagined.
But neither is your power.
And neither is your becoming.
You are not your mother's wounds.
You are not your grandmother's silence.
You are not the grief they never got to name.

You are the first.
You are the healer.
You are the reckoning.
You are the release.
You are the bridge between what they survived
and what your children will never have to carry.

And because of you—
they will know peace.
They will know freedom.
They will know a different kind of love.
It ends with you.
And because of that, a new story begins.

Reflection Questions

1. What patterns did I inherit that I now reject?
2. What does breaking the cycle look like in my daily life?
3. What legacy am I building for those who come after me?
4. Where do I still feel resistance in releasing inherited wounds?
5. What new belief system am I creating for myself?

Journal Space

Use this page to reflect on the questions—or write what your spirit needs to say.

_____

_____

_____

_____

_____

_____

_____

_____

_____

_____

_____

_____

_____

_____

_____

_____

The Shift *(Interlude)*

It's not just the toxic cycles killing us—
It's the food. The alcohol. The drugs. The silent pain.
The fake peace.
The systems designed to keep us numb.
The trauma still living in our DNA.
And once you start waking up, everything starts to hit different.
Food doesn't taste the same, alcohol starts to taste like poison,
and small talk feels empty.
The heaviness in the room? You can feel it in your chest now.
Your body starts rejecting what your spirit can no longer tolerate
and that's how you know the shift is happening.
You're becoming more aware—
and with that awareness, you start realizing...
I can't keep doing this.

And don't worry if no one else sees it yet.
This shift is yours.
You're not here to change them.
Just observe, witness the patterns, and let your awareness guide
you.
There's going to come a moment when you're in a room you've
been in a thousand times—
and suddenly, your spirit just says, no.

No to the heaviness.
No to the fake smiles.
No to the passive-aggressive questions.
No to the "jokes" that leave you bleeding inside.

You'll be sitting at a birthday party, a holiday dinner, a Sunday
gathering—
and you'll feel it.
The same energy.
The same roles.
The same people saying the same shit that always cuts too deep.

Your siblings making fun of you.
Your mother watching you like a hawk, judging your every move.
Your father belittling you in front of everyone, but calling it "just how he talks."
The aunties whispering about your weight.
The cousins side-eyeing your healing like it's a performance.
Nobody sees you.
But everyone has something to say about you.
And you'll sit there thinking...
Why am I still doing this to myself?

You're not crazy.
You're not dramatic.
You're not weak.
You're just finally done.

Done tolerating emotional abuse dressed up as "family."
Done being the punchline.
Done performing.
Done overcompensating.
Done pretending this dysfunction is love.

And let's talk about the other shit, too.

The way we show up to every gathering with plates full of food that's killing us.
Heavy-ass meals passed down like trauma—
seasoned with grief and served with silence.
The way folks pour liquor shots just to feel something or nothing.
Drunk-ass uncles and drunk-ass cousins passing around the pain like it's tradition.
We numb. We eat. We spiral.
And then, we call it culture like it's sacred—
when really, it's just survival on autopilot.
It's all connected—
the food, the silence, the chaos, the shame.
And you don't have to carry any of it anymore.

Let me say this clearly:
You don't have to keep showing up to be torn apart.

You don't have to prove your worth to people committed to misunderstanding you.
You don't have to play the role they wrote for you when you were eight.
You don't have to sit through the gaslighting, the guilt-tripping, the emotional manipulation.

You can leave.
You can reclaim your peace.
You can redefine family.
You can love people and still love yourself more.

And yes, it'll be messy—
you'll grieve, and there will be moments you second-guess yourself because they've trained you to doubt your intuition.

But baby, that's the shift.
The moment when you realize, you don't have to sit there and bleed just because y'all share blood.
If you're sitting in a room that no longer feels safe and your spirit goes quiet every time they speak to you.
If you leave feeling smaller, heavier, and more disconnected every time—
that's your sign.

You are allowed to outgrow the version of you they still expect to see.
You are allowed to set boundaries with people who call it betrayal.
You are allowed to protect your peace without a permission slip.
You are allowed to choose yourself.

Even when it makes the room uncomfortable.
And it's not always loud.
Sometimes, it looks like staying home.
Not texting back.
Saying less.
And walking out without making a scene.

Let the shift happen.
Let it be awkward.

Let it be silent.
Let it be loud when it needs to be.

Let it cost you what it must—
because anything that falls away wasn't meant to hold
the version of you you're becoming.

It's not just about leaving the certain people or places.
It's about leaving the version of you
who thought you had to stay.

The shift isn't punishment.
It's permission.
Permission to heal.
Permission to choose peace.
Permission to be new.

Chapter 3: Shadow Work

There comes a moment in every woman's journey
when she can no longer outrun herself.
No relationship, no job, no achievement, no amount of
pretending —
will silence the whisper inside.
A whisper that says:
There is something here you haven't faced.
At first, you ignore it.
You scroll.
You stay busy.
You fill your calendar, your online shopping cart, your glass.
You chase love that doesn't nourish.
You wear the mask that keeps everyone comfortable.
You tell yourself you're fine.
That it's nothing.
That you're just tired.
That this is what being a woman feels like.

But it lingers.

And the more you resist, the louder it becomes.
This is the call to shadow work.

What is the Shadow?

The shadow is the part of you that was pushed into the darkness.
The wounds you never acknowledged, the beliefs you inherited
but never questioned, and the emotions you were taught to
suppress.

Your shadow holds:
- The childhood wounds you pretend don't still hurt.
- The fears you cover up with strength.
- The emotions you were never allowed to express.
- The patterns that keep repeating in your life because you haven't addressed their root cause.

Your shadow is not your enemy.
It is not something to be destroyed, it is something to be integrated.
Shadow work isn't about erasing your darkness.
It's about learning from it.
Meeting yourself fully—
without shame, without judgment, without rejection.

The First Time I Met My Shadow

I will never forget the first time I unintentionally did shadow work.
I was in my car.
It felt like everything was closing in.
I couldn't breathe.
And my thoughts were turning dark.

"What's the point?"
"Why am I still here?"

I didn't feel like I was living—
I was just here, holding on for *her*.
The only reason I hadn't given up completely was because I didn't want my daughter to lose both of her parents.

At that time, anxiety ruled my life—
it dictated how I moved, how I thought, how I showed up in the world.

And that day, it felt unbearable.
But instead of trying to push it away, I did something different.
I talked to it.
Like it wasn't just a feeling—
but a separate entity.

"What do you need from me?" I asked.
"What are you trying to tell me?"

I had never spoken to my emotions this way before.
And suddenly, I felt a shift.
My anxiety responded—
not in words, but in sensation… in awareness.
It didn't need to be fought, silenced, or avoided—
it just needed to be acknowledged.
So I said,
"I see you.
But right now, I need to focus.
Can you go back on the shelf for a moment?
And we can deal with this later."

And just like that, it eased.
The weight lifted.
That was the day I learned—
my shadow was not my enemy.
It was my messenger.

Before You Begin Shadow Work

Healing doesn't look like posting about it on Facebook for likes
and applause.
It doesn't look like making announcements every time you feel
something.

Real healing gets quiet.
It gets uncomfortable.
It pulls you inward—
into the parts of yourself you've spent years trying not to face.
Curiosity is the first step.
The kind that gets still.
The kind that goes inward and asks:
Why do I respond like this?
Why does this keep showing up in my life?
What haven't I grieved yet?

That's the work.

Everybody wants healing until it starts asking something of them.
Until it starts pulling back the layers, removing the excuses,
showing them the mirror.
People want the vibe, not the transformation.
Because baby, when you really want it?
You lean in.
You ask the hard questions.
You wrestle with it.
You've got to chase the fire—
and not worry about getting burned by it.

How to Begin Shadow Work

Shadow work is not easy, it is deep, uncomfortable, and at times—
painful. But it is also liberating.

Here's how to begin:

Step 1: Create a Safe Space for Your Emotions
- Shadow work cannot be rushed. It requires a container of safety.

- Find a quiet place where you can be alone.
- Give yourself permission to feel without judgment.

Step 2: Observe Your Triggers
- Every trigger is a teacher.
- When something activates you, ask:
1. What is this bringing up for me?
2. What does this remind me of?
3. Where have I felt this before?

Step 3: Meet Your Shadow with Curiosity, Not Shame
- Instead of saying, "Why am I like this?", ask:
1. What is this part of me trying to protect?
2. What unmet need is underneath this reaction?

Step 4: Dialogue with Your Shadow
- Just like I did that day in my car, try speaking to your emotions.
- Ask them what they need.
- Reassure them that they are seen, safe, and not alone.

Healing the Inner Child

Shadow work often brings us back to childhood.
To the moments we were told:
"Stop crying before I give you something to cry about."
"Stop acting like a girl."
"What the hell is wrong with you."
"You're so damn dramatic."
"You act just like your daddy."
"Ain't nothing wrong with you, you just want attention."

Words that weren't just harsh—
they were training.

Training you to numb.
To shut down.
To silence yourself before anyone else could.
But let's be clear:
You were never too sensitive.
You were never too much.
You were just feeling.
And nobody knew how to hold that.
But here's the truth:
You can give yourself now what you needed then—
the safety, the tenderness, the truth that you were never wrong for
feeling.

Activation

Close your eyes and picture your younger self.
What does she look like? How does she feel?
Imagine holding her.
Whisper to her:

You are safe. You are loved. You are enough.

Write her a letter.
Tell her everything she needed to hear.
The words she waited for. The ones no one ever said.
You get to say them now.

This is reparenting.
This is becoming the love she always needed.
This is how you come home to yourself.

The Gift of Shadow Work

Shadow work isn't about staying stuck in darkness.
It's about *bringing light* to the places you once feared to look.
It's about reclaiming the parts of yourself that were never
broken—just buried.
The parts they told you were "too much."
The parts they punished, silenced, or ignored.
The parts that made you feel unworthy,
when really, they were your power all along.
The more you integrate your shadow, the less it controls you.
The more you meet yourself fully, the less you beg the world to
see you.
You don't have to perform for love anymore.
You don't have to hide your truth to be accepted.
You're not a problem to be fixed.
You're a woman finally returning to herself.

Closing Ritual

If you feel ready, try this practice:

1. Light a candle. Sit in stillness.

2. Write down the parts of you that still carry shame.
   The parts you hide. The parts you silence.

"I was taught to be ashamed of my emotions."
"I have ignored my intuition."
"I have silenced my own voice."

3. One by one, read them aloud and say:

- I see you.
- I honor you.
- I no longer reject you.

4. Burn the paper (safely) or rip it up. Let it be released.

Affirm: *I am worthy of being seen in my fullness.*

Final Words

The deepest love you will ever experience
won't come from another person.
It will come from you—
when you finally choose to meet yourself
in the places you once abandoned.
In the tears you swallowed.
In the anger you buried.
In the truths you were too afraid to speak.

Shadow work isn't about fixing yourself.
It's about *finding* yourself in the rubble.
It's about loving the version of you
that didn't get it right, that lashed out, that shut down, that still
showed up anyway.
This is the work that rewrites your story.
Not by erasing the past—
but by facing it with power and presence.
And everything you meet in the dark
has the power to return you to the light.

Reflection Questions

1. What truth am I still afraid to admit to myself?
2. What childhood wounds still impact me today?
3. How can I meet myself with more compassion and curiosity?
4. What pattern keeps repeating no matter how much I try to change?
5. What part of myself am I ready to reclaim?
6. Where can I offer myself grace I've been waiting to receive from others?

Journal Space

*Use this page to reflect on the questions—or write what your spirit
needs to say.*

_____

_____

_____

_____

_____

_____

_____

_____

_____

_____

_____

_____

_____

_____

_____

_____

_____

_____

Chapter 4: Inner Child Healing

There is a little girl inside of you.
She is still there.
She still carries the wounds of every time she was unheard,
unseen, or made to feel unworthy.
But she is also the key to your freedom.

Inner child healing is the practice of returning to her,
holding her, and giving her everything she needed but never
received.
And when you learn to love her—
when you finally give her the safety and validation she has been
waiting for—
you heal the woman you are today.

The Wounded Inner Child and Her Patterns

The Abandoned Child
- Struggles with feelings of rejection and unworthiness.
- Fears being left behind, so she clings to relationships that don't serve her.
- Overcompensates by proving her worth through doing, giving, or people-pleasing.

The Silenced Child
- Grew up feeling like her voice didn't matter.
- Was often dismissed, told to "be quiet" or "stop being dramatic."
- Struggles to communicate her needs and often feels invisible.

The Overachieving Child
- Learned that love was conditional—only given when she was good or successful.
- Feels like she is never doing enough, even when she accomplishes great things.
- Struggles to rest, feeling guilty when she's not being productive.

The Forgotten Child
- Grew up in chaos or neglect, learning to fend for herself too early.
- Has trouble trusting others or accepting help.
- Often feels like she must do everything on her own.

The Letter to Her

When my therapist first asked me to write a letter to my younger self, I thought it would be easy.
I thought I knew what she needed to hear.
I sat down, pen in hand, and started writing.
But the words felt… flat.

I wrote things like:
"You are strong."
"You are worthy."
"You are enough."

All true, but I wasn't feeling them.
And when I read the letter out loud, my therapist paused.
We both felt it—something wasn't landing.
It was in that moment I realized:
I wasn't fully connecting to my inner child.
There was a blockage.

Not because I didn't care.
Not because I didn't want to heal.
But because there was a part of me that still felt unseen.
A part of me that didn't know how to receive the love I was trying to give.
My therapist asked me to try again.
The next time, I dropped out of my head and into my heart.
Instead of writing what I thought my younger self needed to hear—
I became her.
And suddenly, the words flowed differently.

"I see you."
"You don't have to be silent to be safe."
"You deserved to be supported, even in the small things."
"You were never too much. You were always enough."

This time, the words felt real.
And when I read them out loud, I felt the shift.
This was the moment I realized:
My healing was in being fully seen.
Not just by others—
but by myself.
And now…
I do not silence my truth.
I do not dim my light.
I do not abandon myself.

I fully feel.
I fully express.
I fully honor my own experience.

Because I am the cycle breaker.

And that little girl in me?
She is finally safe.

How to Begin Inner Child Healing

Healing your inner child isn't about blame or being stuck in the past.
It's about freedom. It's about wholeness.
It's about finally becoming the one who never leaves her behind again.
It is about giving yourself now what you needed then.

Step 1: Acknowledge Her Presence
- Close your eyes and imagine your younger self.
- What does she look like?
- What is she feeling?
- What is she still carrying?

Step 2: Speak to Her with Love
- Whisper to her: *"You are safe now."*
- Tell her everything she needed to hear.
- Let her know that she is loved, protected, and never alone.

Step 3: Write Her a Letter
- Start with, "Dear little me…"
- Write to her as if she is real—because she is.
- Tell her the things she longed to hear.
- Let her know she is enough.

Step 4: Give Her What She Missed
- Did she need more play? Start incorporating joy into your daily life.

- Did she need more safety? Create rituals that make you feel grounded and secure.
- Did she need more love? Practice deep self-compassion.

The Reparenting Process

Reparenting is the process of becoming the loving, nurturing, supportive figure that your inner child needed.

It means:
- Speaking to yourself with kindness, instead of criticism.
- Validating your emotions, instead of dismissing them.
- Setting healthy boundaries, instead of abandoning yourself for approval.

Affirmation: *I am now the mother I needed. I give myself permission to be free.*

Activation

Try this tonight:
Sit in stillness. Close your eyes.
Imagine your younger self standing before you.
Hold her hand. Look into her eyes.
Whisper to her:

You are safe now.
You are deeply loved.
I will never abandon you.

Let her dissolve into you, integrating into your heart.
Let this be the moment you finally bring her home.

Shadow Work Integration

There's a part of you that still defends the people who hurt you.
A part of you that whispers, "They did their best."
And maybe they did. But that does not erase what you lacked.
You were a child.
You deserved safety.
You deserved to be seen.
You deserved love that didn't come with conditions.
If you feel resistance to reparenting yourself, sit with that discomfort.

Ask yourself:
- Where do I still excuse the pain I endured?
- Why do I feel guilty for needing what I never received?
- Have I mistaken neglect for strength? Have I learned to wear my wounds like armor instead of healing them?
- Do I believe that receiving love now means betraying the people who couldn't give it to me before?

Your inner child does not need you to justify the past.
She needs you to see her, hold her, and give her the love she waited for.
Will you finally answer her?

Final Words

Your inner child is not broken.
She was never unworthy.
She was just waiting for someone to see her, to hold her, and to remind her that she was always enough.
And now—
you are that person.

This is your moment to release the past and reclaim your power.

You don't have to earn your healing.
You don't have to prove you're worthy of it.
You were always enough—
even before you knew how to love yourself this way.
And now, every time you choose yourself, every time you speak to yourself with tenderness, every time you hold your inner child with compassion—
you are rewriting the story.

Reflection Questions

1. What does my inner child still need from me?
2. What limiting beliefs did I inherit from childhood that no longer serve me?
3. How can I incorporate more play, joy, and lightness into my life?
4. What would change if I spoke to myself the way I needed to be spoken to as a child?
5. How can I commit to reparenting myself with love, patience, and care?

Journal Space

Use this page to reflect on the questions—or write what your spirit needs to say.

_____

_____

_____

_____

_____

_____

_____

_____

_____

_____

_____

_____

_____

_____

_____

_____

_____

_____

_____

_____

Chapter 5: The Ache of Motherhood

I need you to know something before you read this.

This was the last chapter I wrote.

But you're not going to find it at the end of the book.

No, this chapter belongs right here—

in the middle of your journey.

In the messy middle where you're still digging, still unraveling, still healing.

I'm only telling you when this chapter was written because I need you to understand that healing is not linear.

Alignment doesn't mean you stop aching.

Awakening doesn't mean you never collapse again.

And this chapter was born during a storm—

an emotional one.

It was a Thursday.

And out of nowhere… the ache returned.

The same ache I carried when I was pregnant and alone.

The same ache I felt in the hospital room, deciding not to call him.

The same ache that showed up again—

on her first birthday,

her second,

and then her third.

It came back.

And this time, it brought exhaustion so heavy that my body gave out.

And then came the nausea.

That's when I knew—

this wasn't just emotional, it was physical.

I had eaten food completely out of alignment with what my body actually needed—

fried chicken and overly sweet lemonade, and it hit me like a wave.

Not just in my stomach.

In my spirit.
Even though I'd spent the entire day pouring—
giving, writing, and showing up...
I had been neglecting *me*.
And Spirit checked me through my body.
This is what happens when you try to keep giving
while bypassing what your body is asking for.

I paused.

I took medicine, asked for family for help, and let myself collapse.
And when I finally slowed down enough to honor what my body
really needed—
I got in the shower.
That's when this chapter dropped in.
That's when I realized—
I had to live it to write it.
This chapter is about what it means to ache in a body that's still
trying to show up.
It's about being soul tired and still feeling guilty for resting.
It's about being deep in your spiritual walk and still unraveling
sometimes.
This chapter belongs in the middle of the book—
because that's when this usually happens.
When you think you've reached a new level,
when you think you're past all of the messiness...
and then out of nowhere, the ache returns.
And your body says:
We're not done yet, there's still something here.

Think of it like this—
The beginning of this book? That's your shadow work, your
processing.

The middle? That's reclamation, that's you getting clear on who the hell you are.

The end? That's embodiment. That's integration.

That's you walking in your power.

But *this* chapter?

This is the reminder that the ache can show up in all three.

And it doesn't mean you're doing it wrong.

It means you're doing it *real*.

If you're here and you feel like you're breaking down again—

If the sadness, the exhaustion, or the ache has come back out of nowhere—

I need you to know something.

You are not broken.

You're breaking open.

You're not backsliding.

You're meeting yourself at a deeper layer.

You're not ungrateful.

You're finally honest enough to say: this is heavy.

You're being asked to tend to what's been buried.

And that's what this chapter is about.

When the Ache Returns

You might've thought that once you healed, you wouldn't feel this again.

That once you were aligned and grounded, the tears would stop.

The weight would lift.

But here's the truth:

You can be fully healed and still ache sometimes.

You can be spiritually awake and still collapse.

You can love your children with your whole soul.

And still feel like you're disappearing.

Love doesn't erase the ache.
Not the ache of being touched out.
Not the ache of being needed constantly.
Not the ache of disappearing behind the role of "mom" and
forgetting what *you* sound like.
You may be the one everyone turns to.
But sis, under all that strength—
You're still a woman.
And that woman needs tending too.
The ache isn't always loud, sometimes it's quiet.

It shows up like this:
- You haven't washed your hair in weeks, and it doesn't even feel worth doing.
- You scroll past your reflection and barely recognize her.
- You eat whatever's quick—not because you don't care, but because you're tired.
- You stop asking yourself how you feel, because what's the point?
- You hold it together for everyone else, but inside, you're unraveling.

Then it hits you.
The sadness.
The anger.
The resentment.
The ache that whispers:
I miss me.
That moment you realize you've been surviving on autopilot.
But let me remind you of something.
You can grieve and still be a damn good mother.
You can want more and not be ungrateful.
You can be tired of giving and still be full of love.

This ache?
It's not proof that you've failed.
It's an invitation.
To *return to yourself.*

Activation

You've cried, felt, and seen yourself again.
Now you move.
Not fast, not recklessly, and not all at once.
Just one step.
Because this isn't about perfection.
This is about *coming back to you.*

Pick something small:
- Wash your hair.
- Drink some water.
- Put on music and stretch.
- Text someone and say, "I'm not okay."
- Go outside and feel the sun on your face.

You don't need a deep ritual.
You just need a decision—
to show up for you.
That's how you return and how you rise.

Final Words

This chapter was never just about motherhood.
It was about the ache that lives in the bones of every woman
who has ever had to mother herself.

The ache of being the strong one.
The reliable one.
The soft place for everyone else to land—
while silently craving someone to hold you.
This is about the women who learned to self-soothe
because no one else knew how to love them properly.
The women who pour and pour and pour—
and are rarely, if ever, poured into.
And still, we get up every damn day
being everything to everybody.

But hear me when I say this:
You are not just here to be everything for everyone else.
You are not just here to carry it all with grace.
You are here to be held too.
And if no one has held you the way you needed?
Then this is the moment you start learning how to hold yourself.
Tenderly. Honestly. Without guilt. Without apology.
That, too, is motherhood.
And it begins with you.

Reflection Questions

1. Where have I been disappearing in my own life?
2. What does my body need right now that I've been ignoring?
3. When did I last feel like *me*—and what brought me back?
4. Where am I still grieving or carrying unspoken resentment around motherhood?
5. What would it look like to mother myself with the same tenderness I give my child?
6. What kind of help do I need—but haven't asked for?
7. What's one small thing I can do to nourish myself this week—not as a mom, but as a woman?

Journal Space

Use this page to reflect on the questions—or write what your spirit needs to say.

_____

_____

_____

_____

_____

_____

_____

_____

_____

_____

_____

_____

_____

_____

_____

_____

_____

_____

_____

Chapter 6: The Power of Self-Validation

There was a time when my worth was determined by the attention I received.
I sought validation in subtle ways—
how I positioned my body in pictures, carefully crafted my words to be understood, and how I anticipated responses—
waiting for someone to affirm me.
But the moment I awakened to my own power; I realized that validation from others fades...
But self-validation? That's eternal. That's your anchor.
A woman who no longer seeks external approval is *untouchable*.
She is her own source of affirmation, her own muse, her own safe space.
And that is what this chapter is about—
letting go the need to be seen, chosen, or validated by anyone other than yourself.

The Illusion of Validation

We live in a world that thrives on external validation.

From the time we are little girls, we are taught to seek approval:
- To be praised for our beauty, but not too confident.
- To be liked, but not too opinionated.
- To be chosen, but never too unattainable.

It's quiet conditioning—
but powerful. And it teaches us that we're only valuable when someone else decides we are.
But validation is a drug.
The moment you rely on it, you crave more.

You quiet your needs.

You compromise.

You disappear in plain sight.

And before you know it, you've lost sight of yourself entirely.

The Subtle Ways We Seek Approval

Self-validation is not just about "loving yourself."

It's about noticing where you've been outsourcing your worth.

This doesn't always look obvious, sometimes it's disguised as everyday behavior.

Here's how it shows up:

Social Media Validation

- Posting pictures and constantly checking likes.
- Deleting posts if they don't perform well.
- Feeling uneasy when someone doesn't react the way you hoped.

Seeking Male Approval

- Sending revealing pictures or waiting for compliments to feel desired.
- Feeling empty when attention isn't given.

Emotional Triggers

- Feeling anxious when someone doesn't respond.
- Questioning your worth when someone doesn't choose you.

Overexplaining and Overproving

- Feeling the need to justify yourself.
- Seeking to be understood rather than simply being.

People-Pleasing and Over-giving
- Bending over backward to be liked.
- Sacrificing yourself to avoid rejection.

But here is the truth:
A woman who validates herself does not beg to be seen.
She does not perform or negotiate her worth.
Because she is already enough.

Becoming Your Own Source of Validation

The shift from seeking external validation to self-validation
is a process of reprogramming.

Affirm: *My worth is not determined by others. I validate myself.*

Here's how to reclaim your power:

1. Reclaim the Narrative
Every time you seek approval, ask yourself:
- What am I hoping to receive?
- Can I give that to myself?

When you stop outsourcing your worth, you take your power back.

2. Self-Affirmation Ritual
Every morning, stand in front of the mirror and speak words of
validation over yourself. Not just surface-level affirmations—
deep, undeniable truths.

I see you.
You are magnetic, powerful, enough.
You do not need permission to exist fully.

Let this become your daily practice.
Let your reflection become a safe place.

3. Validation Detox
Try this for 7 days:
- No checking social media engagement.
- Sit with discomfort when someone doesn't respond.
- Notice where your worth wavers—and reclaim it.

You will start to feel your own energy returning to you.

Mantra: *I do not explain. I do not wait to be chosen. I choose me, every time.*

Activation

Step 1: Write a Love Letter to Yourself
- Instead of waiting for someone else to affirm you, write the words you've always wanted to hear.

Step 2: Speak It Out Loud
- Read it to yourself. Let it sink in. Notice where resistance comes up.

Step 3: Embody It
- Move through the world as if you have already arrived at full self-validation.
- Watch how the world responds differently to you.

Shadow Work Integration

If you struggle to say no, if you feel guilty for setting boundaries,
if you still seek permission to take up space, ask yourself—
who benefits from this?
Who benefits when you silence yourself?
Who wins when you put their comfort above your own?
Who stays at peace while you abandon yourself?

Because let's be honest—
it was never about whether you are worthy. That was never in
question.
This is about who convinced you that you weren't.
And why you still believe them.
Where did you learn that saying "no" made you selfish?
Who taught you that being agreeable was the only way to be
loved?
Why do you still feel like disappointing others is worse than
disappointing yourself?

And it's not just about people-pleasing.
How else are you outsourcing your validation?
Why do you delete posts if they don't get enough likes?
What does that number mean to you?
Who told you your expression is only valuable if it's seen by
others?
Why do you feel uneasy when someone doesn't respond the way
you hoped?
What are you making their silence mean about you?
Do you believe you are only worthy if others acknowledge you?
Why do you seek attention from men who do not deserve you?
What part of you still needs to be chosen?
Where did you learn that your desirability determines your worth?

Why do you over-explain yourself to be understood?
Who taught you that your truth wasn't valid unless someone else accepted it?
What would change if you believed that being understood was not a requirement for being enough?

Every time you seek validation outside of yourself, you give your power away.
What would happen if you reclaimed it?
What would shift if you no longer needed approval to exist fully?
Who would you become if you finally decided that you are enough, as you are, right now?

You do not owe anyone your exhaustion.
You do not need permission to rest, you never did.
You do not have to prove your worth to be worthy.
This is where you reclaim yourself.
This is where you take back your voice.
This is where you unlearn the lie that your existence is only valuable when it is convenient for others.
Because the truth is?
You were never meant to shape-shift for the comfort of others.
You were meant to be free.

Activation

Tonight, I want you to sit in silence.
Close your eyes.
Place one hand on your heart, one on your belly.
Breathe.
Notice the sensations in your body—
the rise and fall of your breath, the rhythm of your heartbeat.

And when you're ready, whisper to yourself:

I am learning to trust myself again.
I am choosing peace over performance.
I am no longer shrinking to be accepted.
I am becoming the version of me I needed all along.

Feel those words settle into your spirit.
Because you are already everything you've ever needed.

Final Words

You say you don't care what people think—
but you're still with a man who drains you because you're afraid
of how he'll react if you leave.
You still smile at family members who disrespect you because
you're afraid of what they'll say if you set a boundary.
You still entertain friendships that give you nothing—
just so you're not alone.
Let's be honest...
You care.
You care more about being accepted than being at peace.
You care more about keeping the image alive than actually being
free.
You've made comfort your god.
You've made other people's opinions the compass for your life.
But at what cost?
You don't need more time. You don't need more signs.
You don't need another woman to show you how to love yourself.
You need to choose yourself *loudly.*
Because the real flex?
Is loving yourself so much that you'll disappoint *everyone else*
before you ever disappoint you again.

Journal Space

Use this page to reflect on the questions—or write what your spirit needs to say.

_____

_____

_____

_____

_____

_____

_____

_____

_____

_____

_____

_____

_____

_____

_____

_____

_____

_____

_____

_____

Chapter 7: Understanding Energy

There was a time when I believed that reality was something that simply happened to me.
That life was a series of events I had little control over, and my only role was to react.
But as I deepened in my awakening—
I realized everything is energy.
Your thoughts, your emotions, your body, your words, your desires—
all of it is energy.
And the frequency at which you vibrate determines the reality you experience.
Most people move through life unaware.
They wake up each day operating from the same emotional baseline, reacting to whatever the world throws at them—
never realizing that *they* are the ones emitting a frequency that's calling it all in.
But the awakened woman?
She understands her power.
She knows that by shifting her energy, she shifts her entire life.

Energy is Currency

Energy is like money—
where you invest it determines what you receive in return.
If you constantly invest in worry, fear, and doubt, you will receive more experiences that validate those frequencies.
If you invest in gratitude, confidence, and abundance, life will reflect those back to you.
This is why two people can be in the exact same situation and have completely different experiences—
because they are vibrating at completely different frequencies.

Now, where are you spending your energy?

Ask yourself:
- Do my daily thoughts align with the life I desire?
- Am I replaying painful memories or visualizing my future with excitement?
- Am I pouring my energy into people and situations that drain me, or into what nourishes me?

Your life is not random.
It's a mirror.
A reflection of the energy you've been holding—
consciously or unconsciously.

Mantra: *I am intentional with my energy. I invest in the frequency that serves me.*

The Science of Frequency

Every emotion, thought, and belief carries a vibration—
and science backs this up.

In Dr. David Hawkins' *Map of Consciousness*,
he measured the vibrational frequency of different emotional states.
The higher the frequency, the more expanded and magnetic you feel.
The lower the frequency, the more contracted and powerless you become.

Here's a simplified breakdown:
- **Shame and Guilt** (Lowest frequencies) – Energy of self-destruction, fear, and unworthiness.

- **Grief and Fear** – Energy of powerlessness, anxiety, and lack of trust in life.
- **Anger and Pride** – Energy of resistance, fight-or-flight, and ego-driven reactions.
- **Courage and Neutrality** – Energy of openness, possibility, and personal growth.
- **Love, Joy and Peace** (Highest frequencies) – Energy of deep alignment, attraction, and manifestation.

The key to an abundant, magnetic life is operating from a high vibrational state as often as possible.
This doesn't mean you bypass your emotions—
it means you master them.
You learn to feel, to process, and to release, rather than staying stuck in low vibrations.

Reflection
What frequency am I operating from daily?
Is it bringing me closer to or further from the life I desire?

How to Protect and Elevate Your Energy

Now that you understand energy as the foundation of your reality, here's how to keep your vibration high:

Audit Your Energy Drainers
- Who or what is consistently pulling you into a low vibration?
- Are there habits, people, or places that leave you feeling depleted?

Energy vampires exist.
They thrive off your unawareness, but awareness is your weapon.

Cut the cords.

Activation

Write down 3 things that drain your energy.

Awareness is the first step.
But once you see it—
you have to bring your body into alignment too.
Because if your nervous system is in survival, you'll keep leaking energy, even when your mind knows better.

Regulate Your Nervous System
- If your body is constantly in fight or flight, your energy will always feel chaotic.
- Breathwork, meditation, and slow movement bring you back to flow.
- Try this: Inhale deeply for 4 seconds, hold for 4, and exhale for 6. Do this three times and notice the shift.

Affirm: *I am grounded, centered, and in control of my energy.*

Shift from Reaction to Intention
- Instead of waking up and reacting to life, wake up and set the tone.
- Start your morning with a thought that aligns with the frequency you want to carry.
- Example: "Today, I radiate ease and abundance."

Shadow Work Integration

I need you to ask yourself something.
Why do you keep choosing what drains you?
Not from a place of judgment or shame —
but from love.
Because if no one has told you before —
you deserve more than this.

Why do you stay around people who disrupt your peace?
Are you calling it loyalty when it's really self-abandonment?
Do you believe that setting boundaries makes you a bad person?

Why are you still in that roller-coaster relationship, convincing
yourself it's love?
Is it love, or is it an addiction to the highs and lows?
Does the inconsistency make you feel wanted?
Does the chaos make you feel alive?

Why are you staying at a job that drains the life out of you?
Are you afraid of what happens if you finally choose yourself?
Who taught you that security is more important than your well-
being?

Why do you keep saying yes to friends who take advantage of
your kindness?
Do you call it love because it's easier than admitting they wouldn't
do the same for you?
Are you afraid of what happens when you finally say no?
Why do you keep tolerating toxic family dynamics and calling it
love?
Who told you that blood means permission to be disrespected?
What would happen if you finally accepted that "family" is about
energy, not DNA?

Why do you constantly put yourself last and act like it's a noble thing to do?
Who convinced you that your needs come second?
Do you believe that being exhausted and overextended makes you more worthy?

You are not here to prove your worth through pain.
You are here to protect your energy like it's sacred—
because it is.
You are not selfish for choosing peace.
You are not wrong for saying *enough*.
You are allowed to leave spaces that no longer honor you.
This is not about shame. This is about awakening.
You say you want abundance, ease, and alignment.
But do you actually feel safe receiving it?
Because if you've been conditioned to associate struggle with survival, peace might feel like a threat.

What would happen if you finally let yourself expand?
Who would you be if you stopped vibrating at the frequency of *almost* and finally stepped into *overflow*?
What parts of you are still resisting the reality you say you want?

Your frequency is a choice.
Your expansion is waiting.
Are you finally ready to receive it?

Becoming an Energetic Match for Your Desires

Tonight, I want you to try something.
Find a quiet space. Sit comfortably. Close your eyes.
Take a deep breath in.
Feel yourself becoming light. Expansive. Open.

Now, visualize the woman you are becoming.
See her clearly.
Where is she?
What does her life feel like?
How does her energy move through a room?
Now, whisper to yourself:

I am already her.
My energy magnetizes all that is meant for me.
I am aligned, and everything flows with ease.

Hold that energy.
Breathe into it.
Let it settle into your bones.

Because this is how you become the woman who commands her
reality.
This is how you master your energy.
This is how you step into your power.
The moment you understand that your frequency shapes your
reality, you stop striving.
This is the part where you remember—
you had more power all along.

We'll talk more about the difference between control and surrender
a few chapters from now.
But for now, know this:
You were never just a victim to your circumstances.
Your frequency, your energy—
has always been part of what shaped your reality.

And now, you get to choose it on purpose.

Journal Space

Use this page to reflect on the questions—or write what your spirit needs to say.

_____

_____

_____

_____

_____

_____

_____

_____

_____

_____

_____

_____

_____

_____

_____

_____

_____

_____

_____

_____

_____

Chapter 8: Balancing Your Chakras

There comes a point in every awakened woman's journey when
she realizes—
healing is not just about the mind.
It's about the body, the spirit, and the energy flowing through her.
You are not just flesh and bone—
you are energy in motion.
A vessel for life force, divine wisdom, and creation itself.
But when your energy is out of balance, so is your reality.

Your chakras, the seven main energy centers within you—
hold the blueprint of your inner and outer world.
They reveal where you are blocked, overflowing, or disconnected
from yourself.
And when you learn to balance them, you unlock everything:
your power, your peace, your divine flow.

Understanding the Seven Chakras

Each chakra governs a different part of your life—
Not just energy, but your lived experience.
The root of your safety. The spark of your desires.
The fire of your confidence. The openness of your heart.
The courage to speak. The clarity to see.
And the knowing that you are never disconnected from the Divine.

Root Chakra (Muladhara) – I Am
Location: Base of the spine
Governs: Stability, security, and belonging
Signs of Imbalance: Anxiety, financial struggles, feeling
ungrounded, and fear of abandonment

Ways to Balance:
• Grounding exercises (walking barefoot, standing in nature)
• Eating root vegetables
• Affirmation: *I am safe. I am supported. I am grounded.*

Sacral Chakra (Svadhisthana) – I Feel

Location: Below the navel
Governs: Sensuality, creativity, and emotional energy
Signs of Imbalance: Lack of passion, creative blocks, shame around pleasure, and emotional numbness
Ways to Balance:
• Dance, self-pleasure, and creative expression
• Affirmation: *I am sensual. I am creative. I allow myself to feel fully.*

Solar Plexus Chakra (Manipura) – I Do

Location: Above the navel
Governs: Personal power, confidence, and action
Signs of Imbalance: Self-doubt, lack of direction, people-pleasing, and feeling powerless
Ways to Balance:
• Core-strengthening exercises and sun exposure
• Making bold decisions
• Affirmation: *I am powerful. I trust myself. I take up space.*

Heart Chakra (Anahata) – I Love

Location: Center of the chest
Governs: Love, compassion, and relationships
Signs of Imbalance: Fear of intimacy, lack of self-love, difficulty forgiving, and feeling disconnected
Ways to Balance:
• Practicing self-compassion, breathwork, and acts of kindness
• Affirmation: *I am love. I give and receive love freely.*

Throat Chakra (Vishuddha) – I Speak
Location: Throat
Governs: Truth, communication, and self-expression
Signs of Imbalance: Fear of speaking up, feeling misunderstood, over-explaining, and throat tightness
Ways to Balance:
• Singing, speaking your truth, and drinking warm herbal teas
• Affirmation: *I speak with clarity. My truth is valuable.*

Third Eye Chakra (Ajna) – I See
Location: Between the brows
Governs: Intuition, vision, and inner knowing
Signs of Imbalance: Overthinking, self-doubt, struggling to trust your intuition, and lack of clarity
Ways to Balance:
• Meditation, dream journaling, and limiting distractions
• Affirmation: *I trust my intuition. I see clearly.*

Crown Chakra (Sahasrara) – I Know
Location: Top of the head
Governs: Higher consciousness, divine connection, and spiritual awareness
Signs of Imbalance: Feeling lost, disconnected from purpose, and resisting spiritual growth
Ways to Balance:
• Time in solitude, prayer, and surrendering control
• Affirmation: *I am connected. I am divine.*

How I Experienced My Own Chakra Healing

There was a time when I didn't realize my body
was carrying energy it didn't need.
That tension in my shoulders? It wasn't just stress.

It was my heart chakra closing off—
shutting down before it could feel.
That constant need to explain myself?
My throat chakra was blocked.
The anxiety in my stomach?
My solar plexus was screaming for me to step into my power.

But the first time I truly felt my energy shift was during a somatic
release practice.
I had been carrying the weight of old emotions, unspoken words,
and unhealed wounds—
things I didn't even realize were trapped inside me.
And one day, without thinking, I started to shake—
like an animal releasing trauma after a fight.
My body knew what my mind hadn't yet caught up to:
it was time to let it go.
And suddenly, something unlocked.
My shoulders relaxed.
My heart felt lighter.
My breath deepened.
I wasn't just moving—
I was releasing.
Since then, I have honored my chakras through movement, breath,
self-touch, awareness.
Because healing isn't just about thinking differently—
it's about feeling differently.

Energy Rituals

These are the daily rituals I return to when I want to realign and
recharge.

Morning Alignment: Place your hand on each chakra point and
set an intention for balance.

Sacral Activation: Dance, stretch, move your hips—wake up your creative energy.

Solar Plexus Fire: Stand in the sun and feel its power charging your confidence.

Heart Opening: Put your hands over your heart and breathe deeply. Let love in.

Throat Release: Sing, hum, whisper affirmations to keep your truth flowing.

Third Eye Meditation: Close your eyes, place your hands over your forehead, and visualize clarity.

Crown Connection: Spend time in silence. Let divine guidance in.

Shadow Work Integration

Your chakras are not just energy points—
they are mirrors.
They reflect the hidden stories you carry, the wounds you haven't healed, the conditioning that still lingers in your body.

Now, let's get real. Where are you blocked?

Root Chakra (Muladhara) – I Am

Why do you still feel unsafe, even when nothing is threatening you?
Who made you believe that life is about survival, not stability?
Who taught you to operate from fear instead of trust?

Sacral Chakra (Svadhisthana) – I Feel

Why do you suppress your desires?
Who made you feel shame for your sensuality, your pleasure, and your creativity?
Do you genuinely believe you deserve joy, or do you feel guilty when you experience it?

Solar Plexus Chakra (Manipura) – I Do

Why do you question yourself before you even begin?
Who convinced you that confidence was arrogance?
Why do you still hesitate to take up space?

Heart Chakra (Anahata) – I Love

Why do you struggle to let love in?
Who taught you that vulnerability equals weakness?
Are you guarding your heart, or are you blocking your own expansion?

Throat Chakra (Vishuddha) – I Speak

Why do you silence yourself when you have so much to say?
Who made you feel like your voice was a burden?
Why are you still afraid to be fully heard?
What are you afraid might happen if you finally spoke your truth?

Third Eye Chakra (Ajna) – I See

Why do you second-guess your intuition?
Who told you that logic is more trustworthy than your inner knowing?
Why do you ask for signs when you already know the answer?

Crown Chakra (Sahasrara) – I Know

Why do you still doubt your own divinity?
Who convinced you that you are separate from Source?
Why do you seek answers outside of yourself when you are the channel?

Your energy tells a story.
If something feels blocked, it's not random.
There's a reason—a wound, a belief, or a pattern.

Are you ready to see it?

Reclaiming Your Energy

Sit comfortably. Take a deep breath.
Place your hands over your heart. Feel its rhythm.
Whisper:

I honor my body.
I trust my energy.
I am balanced, whole, and in harmony.

Visualize golden light moving through your chakras—
cleansing, clearing, aligning them.
Stay in this energy.
Let yourself be fully present.
Because this... this is your power.

Final Words

Before I began activating my third eye,
I heard all the scary stories.
People talked about seeing things—
shadows, visions, dark energy—
and I'll be honest, it made me hesitate.
But here's what I learned:
You don't need to fear your third eye.
You need to prepare for it.
Before you tap into that level of awareness, you have to be
grounded.
You have to be balanced.
Because without that foundation, the insights can feel like chaos.
This isn't just about *seeing*—
it's about *carrying*.

And if your root, your heart, your solar plexus, and your throat aren't in alignment, what you receive through your crown can destabilize you.

That's why this book didn't start there.

That's why I led you through the layers first.

If you feel tempted to skip ahead or rush the process—

don't.

The way I moved through this journey with intention, with balance, with respect—

is exactly why my activation didn't feel scary.

It felt sacred.

And I want that for you, too.

Move with *reverence*.

Not fear.

Not ego.

Not urgency.

Let your body be ready

before you open the gate.

Reflection Questions

1. What truth have you been swallowing to avoid confrontation or protect someone else's comfort?
2. When was the first time you felt unsafe in your body or in your environment? How might that memory still live in your root chakra?
3. Where in your life do you feel the most shame or hesitation around desire, emotion, or pleasure? What were you taught to believe about those things?
4. In what moments do you notice your heart closing off—do you retreat, overgive, or self-abandon to keep the peace?

Journal Space

Use this page to reflect on the questions—or write what your spirit needs to say.

_____

_____

_____

_____

_____

_____

_____

_____

_____

_____

_____

_____

_____

_____

_____

_____

_____

_____

Chapter 9: Feminine Energy and Magnetism

There comes a moment in every awakened woman's journey
when she realizes she was never meant to chase.
She was never meant to seek validation outside of herself.
She was never meant to overextend herself for anything—
not love, attention, or success.
She was meant to attract.
And the difference between chasing and attracting?
It's the difference between being the fisher and being the ocean.

The Fisher vs. The Ocean

For so long, women have been conditioned to behave like
fishers—
Casting out lines.
Baiting.
Waiting.
Hoping.
And often, settling for whatever bites.
The fisher is always in pursuit—
always strategizing and working for what she desires.
And when she doesn't get the response she wants?
She feels rejected, unworthy, unseen.
But the ocean?
The ocean does not chase.
The ocean simply exists.
And yet, everything—
men, opportunities, wealth, and wisdom—
comes to her.

And because she is vast, deep, and full of life, the fish choose to
swim in her depths.
Some come to the surface and others dive deep.
A few are just passing through.
But the ocean does not cling to any of them.
She remains whole, abundant, and complete.

The Energy of Magnetism

This is what it means to embody feminine magnetism—
to stop casting out energy and instead become the presence that
naturally draws everything toward you.
Magnetism is not about being passive.
It's about being powerful without effort, rooted without reaching.
It is about being so deeply grounded in your power that people
and opportunities naturally gravitate toward you.
It is about living in such energetic alignment that the right people,
the right experiences, and the right love—
everything meant for you, finds its way to you effortlessly.

I remember the moment I first felt this shift within myself—
when I stopped seeking, stopped grasping, and simply allowed.
And the more I let go, the more everything I desired found its way
to me.
You've likely started witnessing this shift in your own life, too.
You've seen how, when you move from desperation to
detachment, the world responds differently to you.
You've seen how, when you no longer seek validation, attention,
or love, it starts seeking you.

What Magnetism Looks Like in Action

You move with ease, not urgency.
The woman who is magnetic is never in a rush.
She trusts divine timing.
She knows that what is meant for her will find her.
She knows that what leaves was never hers to keep.

You let *everyone* reveal themselves.
You no longer prove your worth or convince someone to see you.
Instead, you watch.
You observe.
You allow people to show you who they are—
without trying to control the narrative.
You stop over-explaining and over-giving.
The ocean does not explain its depths.
It does not negotiate its existence.
It does not demand anyone to stay.
And neither do you.

You shift from "What can I do to make them stay?"
to "Are they worthy of my energy?"

The fisher asks:
"What bait do I need?"
"What do I need to say or do to keep them interested?"

The ocean asks:
"Are they capable of swimming in my depths?"
"Do they even belong here?"

You master the art of detachment.
You are no longer attached to outcomes—
Whether it's a text, a relationship, a job, or an opportunity.

You trust that whatever is meant to be yours will come with ease.
And whatever falls away was never aligned with you.

Activation

Tonight, return to the mirror—
this time, as the woman who knows.
Not the one still searching.
Look at yourself.
Not just at your face. Not just at your body.
Look at your energy.
Take a deep breath. Roll your shoulders back.
Stand in your full presence.
Now, whisper these words to yourself:

I am the ocean.
I am deeply magnetic.
I do not beg for what is already mine.
I believe that everything aligned with my purpose is flowing to me
naturally.

Let these words sink into your body.
Let them become your truth.

Shadow Work Integration

The ocean does not beg the fish to swim in her waters.
The sun does not prove its worth to be seen.
The flower does not chase the bees—
it simply blooms.
But you? You are still chasing.
And ask yourself why.

Why are you waiting to be chosen when you were born worthy?
Who made you feel like you had to earn love, attention, or presence?
Why do you still believe them?
Why are you holding onto connections that no longer serve you?
Do you fear being alone, or do you fear what it says about you if they leave?
Why do you still over-give, over-explain, or over-prove?
Did someone once make you feel that just *being* wasn't enough?
Are you performing for love instead of simply receiving it?
Why do you struggle to let go?
Is it really about them, or are you afraid to face who you are without them?
What would happen if you stopped chasing altogether?

Sis, this isn't just about romantic partners.
This is about how you've been conditioned to believe that effort equals value.
That struggle equals love.
That waiting to be chosen is somehow noble.
That silence means safety.

But let me tell you something.
The awakened woman does not beg for what she deserves.
She does not shrink to meet others where they stand.
She commands her space.
She magnetizes what aligns with her.
And when something doesn't resonate?
She walks away without hesitation.
That is the difference between a woman
who is magnetic and one who is desperate.

Journal Space

Use this page to reflect on the questions—or write what your spirit needs to say.

Chapter 10: The Art of Surrender

For so long, you believed that control was power.

That if you could just plan enough, work hard enough, or anticipate every possible outcome, you could shape life to your will.

But true power?

It does not come from control.

It comes from surrender.

Surrender is not passivity, weakness, or giving up.

It is the deepest form of trust.

It is standing in the storm and knowing that the winds are guiding you—

not destroying you.

The awakened woman understands that control is an illusion.

It is the ego's attempt to resist the unknown, to cling to certainty, and to avoid discomfort.

But in reality?

The tighter you grip, the more life slips through your fingers.

There is so much more waiting for you on the other side of letting go.

And let's be clear:

Giving up control isn't the same as giving up responsibility.

Surrender isn't handing your life over to some force outside of you.

It's learning to move with the Divine *inside you*.

You're not giving up your power.

You're learning to hold it differently.

Resistance vs. Flow

Control is heavy.

It is rigid, tense, and exhausting.

It keeps you in a state of worry, trying to push for things that are not meant for you, rushing divine timing.

Surrender is light.

It is fluid, trusting, and magnetic.

It allows life to unfold naturally, guiding you into alignment with what is truly meant for you.

Mantra: *I release the illusion of control. I choose peace over pressure.*

Flow doesn't require struggle. It just needs your permission.

The Energy of Resistance vs. The Energy of Flow

Control (Resistance) vs. Surrender (Flow)

Control (Resistance)	Surrender (Flow)
Forcing things to happen	Allowing things to align
Overanalyzing every detail	Trusting intuitive nudges
Fear of uncertainty	Peace in the unknown
Needing immediate results	Patience and divine timing
Feeling drained and exhausted	Feeling light and magnetic
Gripping what's already gone	Making space for what's arriving

Where do you see yourself right now?

Shadow Work Integration

Where in your life are you still gripping something that should have been released?

Pause.
Breathe.

Now tell yourself the truth—
Are you forcing a relationship that is no longer aligned?
Do you call it "fighting for love"?
Or are you just afraid to let go?

Are you clinging to a job, a friendship, or a version of yourself that
is draining you?
Are you mistaking attachment for loyalty?
Or is it the fear of what your life might look like without the
familiar pain?

Does the unknown make you hesitate?
Do you fear letting go because you can't yet see what's on the
other side?
Do you believe that surrender means losing control?
Or are you willing to accept that true control is knowing when to
release?

Here's the truth you need to face:
Surrender is not loss, it is expansion.
Letting go is not failure, it's the doorway.
The things you're clinging to are the ones clogging the path to
everything you've been praying for.

What would happen if you finally trusted
that what is meant for you will never miss you?

Learning to Trust the Flow of the Universe

Surrender is a practice.

It is the ability to say:
- I do not need to control everything to be safe.
- I trust that what is meant for me will find me.
- I release attachment to specific outcomes and allow life to surprise me.

You may have spent years believing that control kept you safe.
But what if your safety was never in control?
What if your safety was in trusting yourself?
Trusting your ability to navigate whatever comes.
Trusting that you are always supported, even when you can't see how.
When you surrender, you step into a new level of ease.
Of alignment.
Of magnetism.
Life begins to unfold for you instead of feeling like something you must constantly fight against.

How to Embody Surrender in Daily Life

If surrender feels difficult for you, start with these practices:

- *Breathe* into Uncertainty
  When fear rises, pause.
  Breathe deeply.
  Say to yourself: *I am safe in the unknown.*

- *Follow* the Path of Least Resistance
  Notice where life is opening doors.
  Walk through them.

- *Let Go* of Forced Timelines
  The universe is never late.
  What's meant for you is already on its way.
  Trust its timing.

- *Affirm:* I trust.
  When control creeps in, meet it with softness.
  Say it again.
  Say it until it softens your grip.

- *Watch* for Synchronicities
  The more you surrender, the more signs you'll see
  that you are on the right path. Not because sign appear
  more — but because now, you're open enough to notice
  them.

The more you lean into trust, the more you will witness the
universe working in your favor.

Activation

Close your eyes. Take a deep breath.
Feel the weight —
the pain, the uncertainty, the fear.
It's been sitting with you for a long time, hasn't it?
Now, imagine yourself standing in front of a door.
This door represents the life waiting for you on the other side of
your pain.
It is sturdy, yet inviting.
You place your hand on the handle, but something inside you
hesitates.
The fear of the unknown...
the comfort of what's familiar —
even if it hurts —
keeps you standing still.

Breathe deeply and remind yourself:

I am my own hero.
I do not need to know the full path to take my first step.
I trust the timing of my life."
I release the version of me that only knew how to survive.
I no longer call it loyalty when it's actually fear.

You walk through the door —
not because you know what's next, but because you trust yourself
to handle whatever meets you there.
As you turn the handle, a warm light spills through the opening.
You don't need to see everything beyond it yet —
you only need to step forward.
You trust that your healing is waiting.
You trust that you are capable of holding yourself through the
journey.

Reflection Questions

1. What is one specific area of your life where you can feel
   yourself gripping too tightly? What would it look like to
   trust instead of control in that area?
2. Where are you still trying to force outcomes out of fear?
3. What part of your identity is still tied to proving your
   worth through struggle? What would happen if you
   released that story?
4. What would freedom feel like if you weren't afraid of what
   it might cost you?

Journal Space

Use this page to reflect on the questions—or write what your spirit needs to say.

Chapter 11: Rituals of the Awakened Woman

There was a time when I viewed sensuality
as something separate from my power—
something reserved for attraction, intimacy, or aesthetics.
But as I deepened in my awakening, I realized that sensuality is
the key to self-mastery.
It's how you experience the world.
How you feel energy.
How you open yourself to receive.
And ultimately, it is the way you *surrender*.
Sensuality is more than just pleasure, it is *presence*.
When you become fully present in your own body, in your own
sensations, you step into a new realm of power.
You begin to see yourself differently:
As magnetic.
As sacred.
As undeniable.
This is when the world begins to respond to you differently.
This is when you shift—
from effort to ease, from control to surrender.
This is where you awaken.

The Art of Sensory Presence

The way you touch yourself, and the way you allow yourself to be
touched—
teaches the world how to treat you.
If you move through life without reverence for your own body,
your own energy, the world will reflect that back to you.
Every time you touch your own skin, whisper to yourself:

I am divine. I am sacred. I am worthy of gentle hands.

Let your own touch be a prayer, a ritual, a moment of deep presence.

Breath as Power

Your breath is the most natural, effortless way to connect with life.
Shallow breaths signal survival mode.
Deep, intentional breaths signal safety and surrender

Practice:
- Place one hand on your belly, one on your chest.
- Inhale deeply through your nose, let your belly expand.
- Exhale slowly through your mouth, releasing tension.
- Feel yourself sinking into your body.

Pleasure as Prayer

Pleasure is not a sin.
It is not selfish.
It is not something you must earn.
Pleasure is your birthright.

Eat with awareness. Let every bite be an experience.
Move with intention. Feel the fabric of your clothes against your skin.
Embrace the moment. Let pleasure exist in the small things:
- The warmth of the sun.
- The sound of rain.
- The way your body feels after stretching.

The more you allow yourself to experience pleasure deeply,
the more you rewire yourself to receive abundance in all areas of
life.

The Ritual of Self-Pleasure

There was a moment when I realized that self-pleasure was more
than just physical release, it was a portal.
A way to channel my deepest desires into my body, into the
universe, into reality itself.
One afternoon, I felt an undeniable pull.
An urge to release, to create, to expand.

The new moon was approaching, and I knew that my body was
responding to the energy shift.
So, I surrendered to it.
I set the tone—
soft lighting, a warm atmosphere, the perfect song on repeat.

J. Howell's "Rocket."

I began slowly, deeply.
And even though I only stimulated my clitoris, it felt as if I was
being penetrated—
but not by a physical force.
By energy.
I stared at myself in the mirror.
Not just to see.
But to witness.
To experience myself.

And just before climax, I whispered,
"I am confidently stepping into my millionaire status."

And at that exact moment—
I felt an explosion of energy.
My body trembled.
A tear escaped from my eye.
My entire being surrendered.
I felt the energy rise from my root to my sacral, up to my solar
plexus, through my heart, my throat, my third eye—
until it burst through my crown.

In that moment, I was not just experiencing pleasure—
I was manifesting.
This was not just orgasm.
This was alchemy.
A sacred, undeniable, irreversible activation of my highest reality.
This is what it means to fully surrender to your feminine energy.
To know your power, instead of seeking it.
To embody your desires, instead of wishing for them.
To become your own portal.

This is sensuality as self-mastery.

Sensuality as Creation Energy

When you reconnect with your sensual energy, you reconnect with
your power to create.
Your body is not just a vessel of pleasure—
it is a portal.
The same energy that brings you to climax is the energy that
brings your visions to life.

Manifestation isn't about wishing.
It's about embodying.

It's about aligning your body, your mind, and your spirit with the energy of what you desire.

The more you allow yourself to feel, the more you allow yourself to receive.

Pleasure opens the channel.

Presence keeps it open.

Desire moves the current.

This is why an awakened woman becomes magnetic.

She's not chasing life.

She's creating it.

A woman who is fully in tune with her senses, her body, her energy—

She doesn't pursue.

She magnetizes.

She moves differently.

When you cultivate your sensuality, you activate your magnetism.

This is not about external beauty.

It is about embodied confidence.

This is not about trying to be seen.

It is about knowing you are unforgettable.

The more present you become, the more life begins to align with your essence.

Shadow Work Integration

Before we close this chapter, I want you to pause.

How did this chapter make you feel?

Did it make you uncomfortable?

Did you feel resistance rising in your body?

Did you find yourself shifting in your seat, avoiding certain sentences, skimming past the parts that felt too bold?

If so, good.

That discomfort? That is your shadow speaking.
And this is where your work begins.

Ask yourself:
- Who told me that a woman speaking about pleasure is unacceptable?
- Why have I accepted that belief without question?
- Have I been conditioned to suppress my sensuality, or is this something I truly believe?

This entire journey—
the journey of the awakened woman—
is about questioning, unlearning, and reclaiming.
If this chapter stirred something inside you, sit with that feeling.
Do not run from it.
Because this is the work.
This is shadow work in real time.
And you are ready for it.

Closing Ritual

Tonight, I want you to create a moment just for yourself.
Run a warm bath. Light a candle.
Put on music that makes you feel sensual and alive.
Touch your own skin. Admire yourself.
Feel your softness. Your warmth. Your presence.
Close your eyes and whisper:

I am the embodiment of power and surrender.
I trust. I magnetize. I allow.
I am fully in my body, fully in my energy, fully in my truth.

The woman who knows her body knows her power.
Move like it.

Reflection Questions

1. How does my body respond when I allow myself to slow down and be fully present?
2. Where in my life am I still resisting pleasure or blocking myself from receiving?
3. What shifts when I trust that I don't have to control outcomes?
4. How can I bring more intentional sensuality into my daily life?

Journal Space

Use this page to reflect on the questions—or write what your spirit needs to say.

_____

_____

_____

_____

_____

_____

_____

_____

_____

_____

_____

_____

_____

_____

_____

_____

_____

_____

The Sky Reminds Me *(Interlude)*

Not all rituals look like incense and altars.
Mine begins 14,000 feet in the air.
The first time I jumped, it wasn't intentional.
I was just checking off a box on my bucket list.
But the second time?
It became a return. A release. A ritual.
There's this moment, right before the fall—
when your toes hang off the edge of the plane.
You feel the wind slap your face.
You see nothing but sky.
The world goes quiet.
And the instructor next to you says,
"One..."
"Two..."

But you never hear three.

Because before he finishes counting, you're already tilting
forward.
Already surrendering.
And the second your body leaves the plane...
your soul lets go.
A lot of people think they'll feel terror when they jump.
But that's not what happens.
You feel surrender.
You feel stillness.
You feel... light.
Your body, your soul, your mind—
everything becomes weightless.
It's not fear. It's flight.

I don't need pews or pages.
My cathedral is the sky.
My altar is the edge of the door.
My release is the fall.
And my prayer is to trust that the universe will catch me
after I've already let go.

I meet God in the freefall.

And right there, midair, I always whisper:

"I release what's heavy.
I trust the universe will carry me."

That's what skydiving is to me.
A sacred practice. A personal ceremony.
A ritual that reminds me I don't have to hold it all.
Because the sky holds me too.

Maybe you don't need a plane.
Maybe you just need a moment—
where you let go without knowing if you'll be caught.
Where you leap anyway.
Where you remember:
The surrender is the prayer.
The freefall is the faith.

Chapter 12: Emotional Alchemy

Every woman has walked through fire.
Some fires burned her.
Some refined her.
Some tried to consume her.
But the real ones—
they awakened her.
One thing is certain:
she was never meant to be destroyed by the flames.

Emotional alchemy is the process of turning your pain into power.
It is the ability to sit with your emotions—
not as a victim, but as a vessel for transformation.
It is the moment you realize:
the heartbreak, the disappointment, the rage, the grief—
none of it came to break you.
It came to teach you.
To strengthen you.
To push you into your next level.

Most people are ruled by their emotions.
They react without thinking, avoid discomfort, numb themselves
with distractions.
But the awakened woman?
She does not run from her emotions.
She meets them.
She listens.
She asks them what they need.
And most importantly—
she learns how to alchemize them.
Emotional mastery is not about avoiding emotions.
It is about working with them, rather than against them.

When sadness visits, she doesn't drown in it—
she reflects and allows it to teach her.
When anger rises, she doesn't become it—
she channels it into motion, into truth, into power.
Instead of being paralyzed by fear, she lets it become her guide.
Your emotions are messengers—
not your identity.

Mantra: *I am not my emotions. I am the alchemist.*

The Process of Emotional Alchemy

1. **Awareness**—Witnessing the Emotion Without Judgment
Most people get stuck in emotional loops because they do not pause long enough to observe what they are feeling.

Ask yourself:
- What emotion is rising in me right now?
- Where do I feel it in my body?
- What is it here to teach me?

2. **Acceptance**—Allowing the Emotion to Exist Without Resistance
The more you reject what you feel, the louder it becomes.
But when you embrace it with compassion, it begins to soften.

Say: *I welcome this feeling without fear. I'm listening.*

3. **Transmutation**—Turning the Emotion into Power
Once you witness and welcome your emotion, you have the power to shift it.

If you are feeling anger—
Move your body.
Let it fuel you.
Take action.
If you are feeling grief—
Write it out.
Let the words cleanse you.
If you are feeling fear—
Breathe deeply.
Remind yourself:

I am safe. I am in control.

Emotions are energy.
And energy?
It can always be transformed.

Activation

The next time a strong emotion arises, instead of reacting, pause.
Ask: How can I turn this into power?

Shadow Work Integration

Most people are not in control of their emotions.
Their emotions control them.
And I need you to ask yourself—
how are your emotions controlling you?
Do you let your triggers dictate your reactions?
When someone upsets you, do you lash out, shut down, or spiral
into overthinking?
Or do you pause, observe, and choose your response with wisdom?

Do you use your emotions as an excuse to stay stuck?
Do you tell yourself, "I can't move forward because I'm still hurt"?
Or do you recognize that healing and movement can happen at the same time?
Are you addicted to your suffering?
Be honest—
Do you replay the same painful memories, over and over?
Do you keep telling the same story—
of how you were wronged, betrayed, abandoned—
instead of choosing to rewrite the narrative?
Do you suppress emotions instead of processing them?
Are you holding onto old anger, grief, or fear because you're afraid of what happens if you actually sit with it?
Are your emotions controlling your decisions?
Do you make choices from a place of fear, insecurity, or past pain?
Or do you operate from wisdom and alignment?

Because here's the truth:
You are not meant to be at the mercy of your emotions.
Your emotions are here to serve you.
But they will only serve you if you learn how to master them.

Releasing Old Emotional Patterns

Most of our emotional responses aren't new.
They are learned.
They are conditioned.
They are recycled.
If you keep finding yourself stuck in the same emotional cycles—
getting triggered by the same things, repeating the same toxic patterns, feeling the same wounds rise again and again—
it's because something deeper still needs to be healed.

Ask yourself:
- Where in my life do I feel stuck emotionally?
- What is the root belief behind this feeling?
- What would change if I finally let this go?

To break the cycle, you must be willing to release what no longer serves you.

Mantra: *I release the emotions, beliefs, and patterns that no longer align with my highest self.*

Closing Ritual

Tonight, we release.
Light a candle.
Sit with yourself in stillness.
Close your eyes and bring to mind the heaviest emotion you've been holding onto.
Place your hands over your heart and whisper:

I feel you.
I see you.
I release you.

As you exhale, imagine the emotion leaving your body—
rising into the flames, being transmuted into light.

Final Words

This might be the hardest part of the journey.
Learning how to sit with everything you feel—
without judgment.

We were taught that some emotions were bad.
That sadness was weakness.
That anger made us dangerous.
That grief should be hidden, and fear should be silenced.
So we labeled them "negative."
And every time they rose, we tried to push them away.

But here, you've been offered a new perspective.
One that doesn't require you to run.
One that invites you to feel it all—
and still choose yourself.
Emotional alchemy is not about avoiding the mess.
It's about meeting it with open eyes, open hands, and a willingness to transform.

Reflection Questions

1. What painful experience in my life has shaped me the most?
2. How do I currently handle strong emotions? Do I react, suppress, or alchemize them?
3. What emotional patterns do I see repeating in my life? Where do they come from?
4. How can I begin to work with my emotions rather than against them?
5. What emotion am I most afraid to feel? Why?
6. How would my life change if I fully mastered my emotions?

Journal Space

Use this page to reflect on the questions—or write what your spirit needs to say.

_____

_____

_____

_____

_____

_____

_____

_____

_____

_____

_____

_____

_____

_____

_____

_____

_____

Sacral Leadership *(Interlude)*

I am the *temple*—
because people feel safe with me.
I'm where they come to be held, to feel a sense of belonging, to
remember they're not alone.
I hold space for community, for truth, for transformation.

I am the *altar*—
because I'm where people lay their burdens down.
They leave feeling lighter, not because I saved them, but because
my presence made it safe to release what they've been carrying.

I am the offering—
because of what I bring:
wisdom, truth, care, and love.
My energy nourishes. My presence fills.
Being in my space is not just an experience—
it's a transmission.

I am the *fire*—
because I burn through illusions.
I don't just ask questions, I pull truth forward.
People come undone in my presence because something in them
knows it's time.
I make people get bare.

And here's the truth:
When a woman reaches this level of embodiment, she becomes a
guide—
whether she meant to or not.
This is where sacral leadership begins.

You're no longer just healing for yourself, you're healing for the
collective.
Your wisdom becomes a mirror.
Your growth becomes medicine.
Your presence alone awakens something in others.

This is not about a title.
This is about frequency.

Leadership doesn't always look like holding a microphone or
standing at the front of the room.
Sometimes it looks like walking through life so anchored in truth
that others feel safe to come undone in your presence.
When you embody this kind of energy, you carry sacred
responsibility.
Because people will come to you unspoken, unannounced—
drawn not to your image, but to your essence.
And you must hold that with care.

You don't owe anyone your energy.
We've already made that clear.
But if someone comes to you, truly seeking transformation—
and you feel called to pour into them, understand the sacredness of
that moment.

You're not saving them.
You're not carrying them.
You're simply honoring the light you carry, and answering the call
when it's real.
The people meant for you don't need convincing.
Your energy is the invitation.
Your embodiment is the doorway.

Chapter 13: Boundaries and Discernment

There comes a point in your awakening when you realize
that not everyone is meant to have access to you.
The version of you who overextended, said yes when she wanted
to say no, and tolerated mistreatment out of fear?

She no longer exists.

And as you rise into this next level, your boundaries become your
shield.
But here's where most women get it wrong:
Boundaries are not walls meant to keep love out.
They are doors meant to invite only the right people in.
Boundaries are not an act of selfishness.
Boundaries are an act of self-respect.
And the ones who struggle with your boundaries are the ones who
benefited from you having none.
And it doesn't need to be shouted from a megaphone or posted on
social media that you're "standing on business."
Your silence will be your power most of the time.
Your energy will say it for you.
And when it's time for it to be loud?
You'll know.
It'll be a "they got me fucked up" moment—
and you'll let them have it.

The High Priestess Energy

When you step fully into your power, you will notice something—
your energy naturally starts filtering people out.
Suddenly...
the ones who were draining you begin to fall away.

The ones who only wanted access, but never wanted to pour into
you—
become distant.
The ones who thrived on your lack of boundaries start resenting
your self-respect.

Let them go.

Because here's the truth most people don't want to accept:
Your boundaries are not just for strangers, they are for *everyone*.
Family does not get a free pass to disrespect you.
Friends do not get lifetime access just because they were there in
the past.
Love does not excuse mistreatment.
If you don't meet my standard, you don't get to access to me.
I have cut off family.
I have cut off friends.
I will cut off *anyone* who disrupts my peace, who does not respect
my boundaries, who thinks they are entitled to me simply because
of history or bloodline.

That is the power of an awakened woman.

She does not negotiate her worth.
She does not lower her standards for comfort.
She does not make exceptions to her boundaries.

Boundaries don't just protect you from strangers—
they protect your future from anything that doesn't align.
And the ones who are truly meant for you?
They will rise to meet you.

Energetic Awareness

You don't just protect your energy physically—
you protect it spiritually, emotionally, and mentally.

Not everyone who smiles at you has good intentions.
Not everyone who claims to love you is aligned with you.
Not everyone who enters your space deserves to stay.

Discernment is the ability to feel beyond words—
to sense when energy is off *before* you have "proof."
To trust your intuition even when logic tells you otherwise.

Here's how to sharpen your discernment:
1. Watch for patterns, not words.
   If someone repeatedly disrespects your boundaries,
   manipulates situations, or drains your energy, pay
   attention—
   their pattern tells you who they are.

2. Trust the way your body reacts—your nervous system
   never lies.
   If your energy shifts when someone enters the room,
   if your stomach tightens when they speak, that is your body
   telling you something.

3. Listen to silence just as much as words.
   Sometimes what people don't say reveals more than what
   they do.
   Who disappears when you set a boundary?
   Who avoids accountability?
   Their absence speaks volumes.

4. Detach from the need for closure.
   You don't need an apology to move on.
   You don't need them to see your side.
   You don't need validation.
   You just need to choose yourself.

Activation

Stand in front of a mirror. Look yourself in the eyes.
Place your hand over your heart and repeat:

My boundaries are an extension of my self-love.
I do not negotiate my worth. My presence is a privilege. Not a
participation trophy.

Feel those words in your bones.
Let them become part of your being.

Final Words

I know how hard it is to set boundaries.
To say no, even when everything in you knows it's time.
This part of the work isn't easy.
It takes intention.
It takes practice.
So before you move on—
slow down.
Really sit with these questions.

Your *no* will become one of the most sacred things you carry.
And you will have to use it often—
to protect your peace, to honor your growth, to reclaim your
power.

You are not here to be available to everything.
Not every invitation deserves your yes.
Not every connection is meant to be kept.

Discernment is your protection.
And boundaries?
They are not walls.
They are declarations:
This is how I honor my worth.

Reflection Questions

1. Where in my life have I been allowing access to people who drain me?
2. What boundary have I been afraid to enforce, and why?
3. How does my body react when someone crosses a boundary? Do I listen?
4. Who in my life respects my boundaries without resistance? How do they show up differently?
5. What would change in my life if I fully honored my own energy?

Journal Space

Use this page to reflect on the questions—or write what your spirit needs to say.

_____

_____

_____

_____

_____

_____

_____

_____

_____

_____

_____

_____

_____

_____

_____

_____

_____

_____

Chapter 14: Love, Attraction, and Self-Worth

There is a difference between a woman who knows she is
powerful and a woman who embodies that power.
For so long, society has conditioned women to dim themselves—
to be desirable but not too much, to be seen but not too bold,
to be smart but not too intimidating.
And for too long, we listened.
We quieted our voices.
We minimized our presence.
We dimmed our light—
so that others wouldn't feel uncomfortable.
But the awakened woman does not diminish herself.
She takes up space.
She moves with certainty.
She does not need permission to be everything she was destined to
be.

The Energy of a Woman Who Belongs

I have always been small in stature, but my presence?
Unmistakable.
At 5'2, I carry the energy of a stallion—
bold, unshaken, walking with the posture of a woman who trusts
life to carry her.
When I walk—
my head is high, shoulders back, and face relaxed.
I do not move with doubt, I move with certainty.
I do not walk with hesitation, I walk like I belong.
And because of that, the world responds to me differently.
This energy didn't come from validation.

It didn't come from waiting on someone else to affirm my worth.
It came from me deciding who I am.
For so long, women have sought permission—
permission to take up space, to be loud, to be confident, to be powerful.
But you don't need permission to be who you already are.
The woman you are becoming does not play small—
not in relationships, not in business, not in life.

She commands respect without begging for it.
She chooses love without chasing it.
She receives abundance without forcing it.
She embodies power without apology.
She does not hope to be chosen.
She does not hope to be seen.
She knows her worth, and the world adjusts accordingly.

The Truth About Self-Worth and Attraction

The energy you carry shapes the way people treat you.
If you walk into a room apologizing for your presence, people will feel that energy.
If you speak as if your voice doesn't matter, the world will reflect that back to you.
But when you own yourself fully—
when you move like a woman who knows she is valuable, desired, worthy—
everything shifts.

1. Men will rise to meet your standards or fall away.
2. Opportunities will come to you naturally.
3. People will either respect your presence or remove themselves.

The world doesn't bend for the woman who silences her own power.
It gives to the woman who stands in her truth, unshaken.

The Moment I Knew I Was Meant for More

I don't come from a lineage of entrepreneurs—
no one paved the way for me.
Yet, in my early 20s, I embarked on this journey blindly, not knowing it was preparing me for something much bigger.
Now, in my late 20s, as I build another business, I understand what I didn't before:
I was never meant to play small.
My presence alone shifts rooms.
I am the first in my lineage to move like this, but I will not be the last.
This isn't just about business.
This is about owning your power in every area of life.
In relationships.
In friendships.
In leadership.
In self-love.

There is a woman inside of you that refuses to be small.
You feel her.
She speaks in your moments of frustration, when you know you deserve better.
She whispers in your ears when you hesitate to ask for what you want.
She stands taller inside of you every time you choose yourself.
She is waiting for you to fully step into her.

Activation

Tonight, I want you to do this.
Stand in front of a mirror. Look at yourself—
not just your body, but your presence.
Take in your features. Every curve. Every detail.
Straighten your posture. Roll your shoulders back.

Feel the energy of a woman who is fully in her power.
Then, say these words:

I was never meant to play small.
My presence is felt before I even speak.
I walk with certainty. I lead with confidence.
I do not wait for permission. I choose myself, fully and completely.

Walk away from the mirror carrying that energy into the world.

Mantra: *I do not doubt my power. I am a force of nature, moving with ease and confidence. The world adjusts to my presence. Because I am her.*

Final Words

Before you move on, I just want to say this.
Don't get me wrong—
I love a woman who knows she's the shit.
I love a woman who walks like she belongs wherever she is.
But that doesn't mean you need to put other people down.
This isn't about that.
This isn't about outshining anybody or trying to be the biggest
thing in the room.

You ever seen what happens when you bring the flame of one lighter to another?
Sometimes one flame is barely hanging on —
and just a little bit of heat from another lighter brings it back to life.
That's what real power looks like.
You don't have to dim anyone else's light to stand fully in yours.
You can be so deeply in your own power that you remind other women of theirs.
That's the kind of woman you're becoming.

Reflection Questions

1. Where in my life am I still playing small?
2. What would change if I fully stepped into my power?
3. How does my self-worth shape the way I attract love, friendships, and opportunities?
4. What beliefs do I need to release in order to embody my full presence?
5. How can I practice owning my space — physically, emotionally, energetically?
6. If my energy alone could shift rooms, how would I move differently?

Journal Space

Use this page to reflect on the questions—or write what your spirit needs to say.

Chapter 15: Men and Masculine Energy

For centuries, women have been conditioned to orbit around men.
To center them in every aspect of life—
our thoughts, our actions, our aspirations.
Even in conversations about feminine energy, we were taught that
our softness, our surrender, and our nurturing—
should all be in service to them.
But what if I told you that was never the point?
The more I awakened, the more I realized that I had to deprogram
everything I was taught about men and their role in my life.
I was shown that my value was in how well I could support,
nurture, and uplift a man.
That if I wanted to be chosen, I needed to be easy to love.
That submission was the highest virtue of a feminine woman.

But here's the truth:
Most men have no business being submitted to.
Submission requires leadership.
And leadership requires self-mastery.
How the hell are we expected to submit to men who don't even
know themselves?
Who are emotionally stunted, avoidant, and unable to provide
safety—
physically, emotionally, or spiritually?
And yet, they have been taught that they are inherently worthy of
power, of leadership and control—
without doing the work.
And we have been taught to make their comfort our priority.

But no, not anymore.

The Treatment

The most jarring realization I had on my awakening journey was
this:
Men treat women based on how they feel about themselves.
A man who is unhealed will make you feel unworthy.
A man who lacks emotional depth will demand that you swallow
your emotions.
A man who is weak will try to make you feel small so he can feel
bigger in comparison.
If a man sees himself as valuable, he will treat you as valuable.
If he sees himself as broken, he will make you feel like you need
to fix him.
If he sees himself as nothing, he will try to make you feel like
nothing.

Most of these men are not actually looking for love.
They are looking for a mother.
A therapist.
A crutch.
A woman to carry the weight of their unhealed wounds—
so they don't have to.
And for too long, we have obliged.

But that ends now.

We are not here to be their crutch.
We are not their mothers.
We are not their rehabilitation centers.

The awakened woman knows she cannot carry what was never
hers to hold.

The Unlearning

I spent months deprogramming myself from male-centered
conditioning—
from the need to be chosen, approved of, and shaped by the male
gaze.
I mean deep unlearning.
I watched videos. I read articles. I sat with myself and asked:
What do I truly want outside of male validation?
Who am I when I stop shaping myself around what men desire?

And what I realized was wild.
I didn't even want to cook anymore.
Not because I don't enjoy it—
but because standing over that stove reminded me of all the hours I
spent cooking for a man who didn't even like me.
I began to reprogram every part of myself that had been trained to
perform.
And that reprogramming required me to deconstruct every part of
myself that was tied to the male gaze.
I stopped responding immediately to texts.
I stopped contorting myself to be more "palatable."
I stopped explaining myself to men who weren't even listening.
I stopped performing.
And that shit pissed them off.
They all felt that shift in me.
They knew they had lost their grip.
I respond when I want.
I engage when I want.
My life does not revolve around a man—
and if that disrupts them, that's not my problem.

Family Is Not an Exception

And let me be clear—
this isn't just about romantic relationships.
I do not tolerate weak masculine energy from *anyone*.
Not from men I date.
Not from coworkers.
Not from strangers.
Not even from my family.

Imagine a woman who has been riding for a man for over a
decade.
She has given him children, supported him through his lowest
moments, sacrificed parts of herself to build a life with him.
And in return?
He is inconsistent, emotionally unavailable, and avoidant.
He disappears when she needs him the most.
He expects to be the priority, even over his own children.
He demands that she worship him—
not because he is leading, protecting, and providing, but because
his fragile ego requires it.
This is what weak masculinity looks like.
And too many women have been conditioned
to believe that this is just how men are—
that it is our job to fix them.
But to be clear:
Weak men are not our burden to bear.
I have seen too many women drain themselves trying to love a
man into his potential.
I refuse to be one of them.
And you should too.

The Power of Feminine Energy

I used to think the power of the feminine was in nurturing men.
I now know the truth.
The real power of the feminine is in her ability to create, to
receive, to magnetize—
not to fix, not to bend.
When I fully embodied my feminine essence, I didn't feel
weaker—
I felt stronger.
A woman fully in her feminine?
She commands devotion, protection, and reverence.
She does not fix.
She does not beg.
She does not settle for weak men.
She does not make excuses for them.
She does not prioritize their needs above her own.
She does not submit to dysfunction.
Because a man who is truly in his divine masculine
will never ask her to.
And if he can't meet you there?
It's not your burden to teach him.
It's your responsibility to release him.

And hold on—
for those of you thinking you're getting let off the hook just
because you don't date men?
This is for you, too.
It doesn't matter who you date.
If you're still shrinking, bending, or betraying yourself to keep
somebody around—
you're still giving your power away.
This isn't about men.
It's about you.

It's about how deeply you honor yourself, no matter who's standing in front of you.

The Truth About Masculine Energy

Masculine energy isn't about gender.
It's about movement. Structure. Leadership. Action.
Every human being carries both masculine and feminine energies inside of them.
The problem isn't masculine energy itself—
it's the distortion of it.

Divine masculine energy:
- Protects, it doesn't possess.
- Leads with integrity, not ego.
- Creates safety, not fear.

Wounded masculine energy:
- Controls.
- Avoids responsibility.
- Destroys trust through inconsistency and manipulation.

When you learn to recognize the difference, you stop making excuses for behavior that drains you.
You stop shrinking yourself to survive distorted spaces.
You stop carrying what was never your burden.

Shadow Work Integration

Let's get uncomfortable for a second.
It's easy to call out the ways men have failed to step up—
but what about you?

Are you still waiting to be chosen?
Do you feel more valuable when a man desires you?
Do you believe your beauty, your worth, or your femininity is
proven when a man claims you?

Are you addicted to proving yourself?
Do you overextend, over-give, or overcompensate in relationships
hoping that if you just love him harder, he will finally step up?

Do you make excuses for weak masculinity?
When a man shows you who he is—
his avoidance, his lack of emotional depth, his inability to lead—
do you accept it and convince yourself you can handle it?

Are you still measuring your success by your relationship status?
If you were single forever, would you still see yourself as whole?
Would you still believe you are enough, even if no man ever
claims you?

This is where your real work begins.
Because the truth is—
many women who believe they are "high-value"
are still waiting to be validated by men.
Still hoping to be chosen.
Still holding their breath, waiting for a masculine presence to
confirm their worth.
But sis—
you are the validation.
You are the value.
You are not waiting for anyone.
And once you truly believe that—
the entire way you move through this world will change.

Activation

Tonight, affirm yourself:

- I am the center of my own universe.
- I do not exist to make men comfortable.
- I do not submit to unhealed energy.
- I am the prize. The muse. The magic.
- My energy is a privilege—not a consolation prize.

Because you were never meant to orbit around them.
They were meant to rise to meet *you*.

Final Words

You say you don't center men—
but let's talk about the man you're still bending for.
The one you keep defending.
The one who ghosts your needs, but you show up anyway.
The one who hasn't earned your energy, but you give it like it's
free.

You say you've healed—
but your body still tenses when he pulls away.
You still overthink your tone so he doesn't get defensive.

You say you don't center men—
but you keep choosing struggle over solitude.
You keep staying in situationships hoping they evolve.
If the thought of cutting him off makes you anxious—
you're still centering him.
If you measure your femininity by how a man responds to it—
you're still centering him.

If your peace rises and falls based on his attention—
you're still centering him.
You don't get to call yourself free while still waiting to be chosen.
You don't get to post "soft life" quotes while enduring hard love in
private.

So tell the truth.
Not for the internet.
Not for your girls.
For you.

Reflection Questions

1. Where in my life have I been centering someone at the expense of myself?
2. How would my choices shift if I moved from a place of self-fulfillment instead of male validation?
3. What behaviors have I tolerated from someone that I now realize were a reflection of their own self-worth?
4. Where in my life am I still playing into outdated gender roles that do not serve me?
5. How do I feel when I embody my feminine power? How do others respond?

Journal Space

Use this page to reflect on the questions—or write what your spirit needs to say.

_____

_____

_____

_____

_____

_____

_____

_____

_____

_____

_____

_____

_____

_____

_____

_____

_____

Chapter 16: Love Rewritten

For so long, we've been told that love requires sacrifice—
that a woman's highest virtue is her ability to endure.
But an awakened woman knows the truth.
Love is not about losing yourself, it is about expanding yourself.
You are not here to shrink, to bend, to prove your worth.
You are not here to pour endlessly into cups that refuse to be full.
An awakened woman does not chase love—
she embodies love.
And because she embodies love, she does not fear its loss.
She knows love should never be something she has to grip tightly
to keep.
She does not plead for it, control it, or lose herself to hold it.
She loves from a place of abundance—
not scarcity.
And that is what makes her irresistible.

This is How She Moves Now

When a woman knows her worth—
everything about her shifts.
She does not fear walking away.
She does not mistake chemistry for alignment.
She does not let potential blind her to reality.
She does not overstay in places she has outgrown.
She sees clearly.

She no longer asks:
"How can I make him love me?"
"What can I do to keep him?"
"Why won't he choose me?"

Instead, she asks:
"Is this a place where my love can thrive?"
"Does this relationship honor my highest self?"
"Am I receiving as much as I give?"

This is the shift from attachment to sovereignty.

Loving Without Attachment

Attachment says:
"I need you to love me so I can feel whole."

Sovereignty says:
"I am whole, and I choose to share my love with you."

Attachment is fear.
It grips, clings, suffocates.
Sovereignty is trust.
It allows, expands, breathes.
A woman who loves without attachment moves differently.

- She does not mistake love for possession.
She knows that no one belongs to her.
People are free to come, free to go.
And she is at peace either way.

- She does not use love as a means of control.
She does not guilt, manipulate, or beg.
She lets love flow freely, knowing that what is real cannot be forced.

- She does not hold onto what is trying to leave.

She does not fear loss.

She understands that love is never lost, it only transforms.

This is how an awakened woman loves.
Deeply, fiercely —
but never desperately.

The Mirror She Becomes

A woman in her full power is not just different —
she is dangerous to the world's idea of love.
She does not settle for half-hearted efforts.
She does not sacrifice her standards for the sake of
companionship.
She does not lower her frequency to meet someone where they are.
Instead —
she becomes a mirror.
A man will either rise to meet her energy or he will remove
himself from her presence.
She allows herself to be pursued, but never for sport.
She sees beyond words —
she watches actions.
She does not confuse effort with alignment.
She knows that real love should feel like peace, not a battlefield.
When she loves, she loves fully, but she does not lose herself in
the process.
This is the kind of love that shifts the entire dynamic of
relationships.
This is what it means to love as an awakened woman.

Closing Ritual

Tonight, I want you to close your eyes and speak these words:

I am worthy of love that expands me, not drains me.
I release all fear of losing love. Love is always within me, around
me, flowing to me.
I am a woman of deep value, and I move in relationships as such.

Let these words sink into your soul.

Because the truth is—
you were never meant to beg for love.
You were never meant to lose yourself in the process of loving
someone else.
Your light was never meant to be dimmed for someone else's
comfort.
You are here to love freely, deeply, abundantly—
but never at your own expense.

Final Words

If you ever get to a place in this journey where you feel like you're
not connecting with people the way you used to, and you're
tempted to start shrinking again—
just to find a love that feels familiar, just to feel seen again—
pause.

Breathe.

And remember:
You are the source of the love you seek.

You are not waiting to be chosen because you already chose yourself.
And if you remember what I've already taught you—
the right people for you will find their way to you.

Reflection Questions

1. Have I ever mistaken attachment for love? How did it show up in my relationships?
2. Where have I sacrificed my standards in the name of "love"?
3. How would my relationships shift if I moved from a place of abundance instead of lack?
4. What would it look like to fully trust that real love will never require me to abandon myself?
5. In what ways can I embody my sovereignty in love?

Journal Space

Use this page to reflect on the questions—or write what your spirit needs to say

_____

_____

_____

_____

_____

_____

_____

_____

_____

_____

_____

_____

_____

_____

_____

Chapter 17: Sacred Sisterhood

Please don't treat this like just another page in a book.

This is the part where you may want to skim through.

Where your ego might flare up and say, "This doesn't apply to me."

But it does.

If you've awakened—

if you've truly come home to yourself, then you already know not everyone can come with you.

This chapter is a release—

a shedding, a reckoning.

We're taught how to lose lovers.

We're even taught how to grieve family.

But no one teaches us how to grieve friendships.

No one teaches us how to release sisterhoods that no longer feel safe, sacred, or true.

But if you're truly becoming the woman you've prayed to be, you're going to have to let go of the ones who only knew the version of you who didn't love herself yet.

There comes a point on the journey where you stop tolerating low vibrational friendships—

not because you don't care about people, but because the old frequency doesn't fit the new you.

You want to know why you're still drained, still second-guessing yourself?

Look around.

Some of y'all are still keeping sisterhoods that feel more like spiritual shackles.

You're craving connection, but surrounding yourself with the familiar.

And now, you're confusing shared history for soul alignment.

Let me make something clear.

Sisterhood is not just group brunches and girls' nights.

It's not about venting about men who don't love you and gossiping about women who intimidate you.
Sacred sisterhood doesn't entertain your delusions—
it holds you higher.
A sacred sister will look you in the eye and mirror your potential back to you.
She'll call you out without making you feel small.
And when you cry about a vision that hasn't been born yet, she'll already be holding space like it's on its way.

Like a snake shedding its skin, you'll have to release what's old, what's tight, and what's restricting your growth.
And yes, that means friendships too.
You can't grow into your next chapter if you're still clinging to what used to fit.
And what do snakes symbolize?
Rebirth, transformation, renewal, wisdom.
Shedding the old self to reveal the evolved self.
That's what sacred sisterhood demands.
That you shed what no longer aligns so you can rise and remember who you are.
This chapter isn't just about friendship.
It's about embodiment.

To embody sacred sisterhood as an awakened woman is to:
- Be emotionally safe for yourself and others.
- Refuse to shape-shift to maintain connection.
- Let go of comparison and competition as forms of connection.
- Practice open-handed love—loving without attachment or fear.
- Recognize frequency over familiarity.
- Allow grief and still open your heart again.

You become the friend you've been waiting for.
You become the circle you've longed to join.
You become a sacred space for truth, for vulnerability, for vision,
and for fire.

Closing Ritual

Find a quiet place.
You don't need crystals, candles, or incense—
unless that feels aligned.
Just your presence. Just your breath.
Close your eyes. Breathe deeply.
Imagine you're building an altar—
not on a table, but within your body.
Within your heart. Within your womb space.
Whisper this to yourself:

I place trust at the center.
I light a candle for truth.
I offer my ego to the flame.
I open space for soul recognition.
I allow old friendships to return to the earth with grace.
I call in soul-aligned sisters with clarity.
This is my altar. May only love sit here.

When you're ready, write a letter to your past self—
the one who chose friends from fear or survival.
Thank her.
Then write a second letter, calling in the friendships your soul is
ready to receive.

Final Words

By now, you might be thinking—
Damn, this girl wants me to cut everybody off.
But that's not what I'm saying.
I'm here to help you understand the importance of surrounding yourself with people you're actually aligned with—
not because of history, not because of blood, but because of frequency.
And I can't stress this enough:
A lot of people wonder why they can't elevate, why they feel stuck, why their spirit feels heavy.
It's the energy they keep around them.
That's why I've taken you through this journey.
That's why I asked you to put everything under the microscope—
family, friends, lovers, all of it.
Because if you're serious about your awakening, you have to be serious about your environment.
You have to know which connections are watering you and which ones are weighing you down.
This isn't about isolation. This is about elevation.
And you deserve to rise without anything tethering you
to the version of yourself you've already outgrown.

Reflection Questions

1. Where have I allowed fear or survival to dictate my friendships?
2. When have I abandoned myself to maintain connection?
3. Who have I outgrown, and what did that relationship teach me?
4. How do I show up as a safe space for other women?
5. What kind of sisterhood am I calling in, and how can I embody it first?

Journal Space

Use this page to reflect on the questions—or write what your spirit needs to say.

_____

_____

_____

_____

_____

_____

_____

_____

_____

_____

_____

_____

_____

_____

_____

_____

_____

Chapter 18: Stepping Into Your Power

There comes a moment in every awakened woman's journey
when she knows, deep in her bones—
that she was never meant to live an ordinary life.
That her presence, her energy, her voice, her very existence is
meant to shift the world in some way.
This isn't just about career or success.
This is about purpose, alignment, and destiny.

For so long, we've been taught to look for our purpose as if it's
something outside of us, something we must seek.
But the truth?
Purpose isn't found, purpose is remembered.
It was never outside of you, it's been within you all along.
You were born with it, it is embedded in your DNA.
It is the reason your soul chose this lifetime, this path, and this
body.
The only thing stopping you from fully stepping into it is
resistance.
And the moment you release that resistance?
You collapse time.
The moment you trust it's already yours?
The universe bends to meet you.
This is not magic, this is quantum creation.

The Science of Alignment

Quantum physics teaches us that everything is energy.
Every object, every thought, every emotion, every intention—
it's all vibrating energy, sending signals out into the universe.

Energy responds to expectation.
Observation changes reality.
The universe is not fixed—
it is fluid.

In the famous Double-Slit Experiment, scientists found that light
could behave as both a particle and a wave, depending on whether
it was being observed.
The moment someone was watching, the light chose a path.
Now, apply this to your life purpose.
If your energy and attention shape the outcome of what you
experience, then ask yourself:
What reality am I observing?
Am I seeing myself as powerful or as limitless?
Or am I still playing small?
You are not at the mercy of fate.
The universe is responding to who you are being.
If you want to step into your highest purpose, you have to first
align with the version of you who already has it.

The Car Accident

I had heard about quantum leaps before, but I had never felt one in
real-time—
until the day I lost control of my car.
I won't get into the details, but in that moment, *I surrendered*—
completely.
There was no panic, no fear, no resistance.
Just trust.
And in that surrender, something surprising happened.
Within days, I had a new car—
one I didn't even know I needed.

The financial support I had been waiting for to launch my LLC
and nonprofit—

arrived with ease.

Everything shifted.

Not because I forced it, but because I aligned with it.

The thought of receiving a new car had only been a passing
thought.

The idea of starting my nonprofit had only been a vision.

And yet, these things manifested in real-time.

Not through effort, not through struggle—

through alignment.

This is quantum creation in action.

The moment you release control, you collapse time.

The moment you trust, the universe moves instantly.

The moment you become the woman who already has it, it arrives
effortlessly.

This is not luck, this is not coincidence—

this is alignment.

And this is how you step into your purpose with ease.

Becoming Her Is the Purpose

Most people think stepping into their purpose means doing more—
hustling harder, proving themselves.

But quantum physics teaches otherwise.

It's not about doing more.

It's about becoming more.

Your external world simply mirrors your internal shift.

If you're forcing, you're resisting.

If you're grasping, you're doubting.

If you're desperate, you're signaling lack.

But when you fully embody the identity of the woman who
already has it, who already *is* it—
everything rearranges to meet your frequency.
This is how you call in your purpose.

The Four Laws of Quantum Alignment

If you are ready to collapse time and step into your purpose
with ease, here's what you need to do:

1. *Shift* your energy before you see the results—act as if it's
   already happening.
   Embody the version of you who already has what you
   desire.

2. *Observe* without attachment—just like the double-slit
   experiment, your observation influences outcomes.
   But if you watch with desperation, you disrupt the process.

3. *Let go* of "How" and focus on "Who."
   Who do you need to be to align with your purpose?
   Quantum shifts happen when you become the energy of the
   reality you want to attract.

4. *Trust*—fully, completely, without fear.
   The moment you surrender, the field responds instantly.

Closing Ritual

Find a quiet space where you can be still.
Close your eyes. Take a deep breath.
Visualize the version of you that already has what you desire.

See her, feel her energy, and become her.
Now, whisper these words:

I surrender to the infinite flow of the universe.
I am aligned with my highest purpose.
I trust the process and release the need to control.
Everything I need is already on its way to me.

Let these words settle into your spirit.
Because the moment you truly believe them, your world will never be the same.

Final Words

You were never here to chase your destiny.
You are the doorway.
You are the signal.
You are the shift.
When you trust who you are becoming—
the world around you has no choice but to respond.

Reflection Questions

1. Where in my life am I still gripping too tightly?
2. How can I shift my energy to match the reality I desire?
3. What would happen if I let go of control and trusted the process?
4. How has the universe already shown me that alignment happens when I surrender?
5. What does it feel like to be in full trust, full surrender?

Journal Space

Use this page to reflect on the questions—or write what your spirit needs to say.

_____

_____

_____

_____

_____

_____

_____

_____

_____

_____

_____

_____

_____

_____

_____

_____

_____

_____

_____

_____

_____

Chapter 19: Stepping into Overflow

For too long, women have been conditioned to believe that success must come at the cost of exhaustion—
that we must sacrifice our peace, our softness, and sometimes even our integrity to "make it."
We've been told that struggle is a rite of passage.
That overworking is a badge of honor.
That hustle is the only way to build wealth.
But awakened women know better.
True success—
the kind that nourishes your soul and creates overflow—
is rooted in alignment.
It's the understanding that what is meant for you flows to you naturally.
It's the trust that when you step into your purpose, the universe clears the path.
It's the knowing that wealth is not just about money—
it's about energy, ease, and expansion.
And *this* is the shift that changes everything.

What Does Alignment Feel Like?

Alignment isn't butterflies.
It's not nervous excitement.
That's anxiety dressed up in disguise.
Alignment is calm.
It's certainty—
a deep knowing in your bones that you are exactly where you're supposed to be.
It feels like the universe is orchestrating everything on your behalf.
When I feel aligned, I feel at peace.
I'm not chasing. I'm not grasping.

I'm flowing.
I feel grounded in my purpose, clear in my energy, and anchored in the moment.
When I'm out of alignment?
I feel it immediately.
I start overextending.
I begin forcing, grasping, doubting.
My well runs dry.
My energy depletes.
And no matter how much I do—
something still feels off.
I used to push through that feeling.
I thought I needed to try harder, hustle more, work longer hours.
Now?
I listen.
And when something is truly meant for you, it will align effortlessly.

The Lie We Were Told About Success

I believed that the harder I worked, the more money I would make.
That was a lie.
I thought I had to grind my way to success.
That I had to constantly to push, to sacrifice to get where I wanted to be.
I even worked in a male-dominated industry, selling cars, where the pressure to perform was relentless.
I was surrounded by men who thrived in the chaos, in the fast-talking, fast-moving world of sales.
I was drained—
my nervous system shot, my body was telling me every day *this* was not it.

And when I finally walked away from that world, I realized success was never supposed to be a fight.
I didn't start attracting true success until I stopped chasing it.
I didn't start making money with ease until I stopped approaching it with a scarcity mindset.
I didn't step into abundance until I truly believed I was already enough.

How to Build Success

If there's one thing I wish more women understood about success, it's this:
You do not have to fight for what is already yours.
The life you desire already exists—
in another timeline, in another frequency.
The only thing standing between you and that life is the belief that you have to struggle to get there.
So instead of asking: *What do I need to do?*
Ask yourself: *Who do I need to become?*

When I stopped chasing and started embodying my highest self, the universe did the rest.
When I surrendered, opportunities aligned with ease.
When I stopped seeing money as something I had to grind for,
I began to see it as something that responds to my energy.
This is why I always say:
"I am a passenger princess, and the universe loves to take care of me."
Because when I lean back and trust—
the universe does the heavy lifting.

Mantra: *I am aligned, magnetic, and deeply supported. I release the need to hustle for what is already mine.*

The Science of Abundance

Most people think money follows hard work.
But in reality—money follows energy.
Approach wealth with scarcity, desperation, or fear, and it will always feel like it's slipping through your fingers.
Approach wealth with confidence, ease, and gratitude, and it begins to multiply.
This is not wishful thinking—
this is quantum physics.
The moment I stopped saying, "I need more money," and started saying, "I have enough. I am provided for. I am supported."
Money began to flow.
Why?
Because when you operate from lack, you create more lack.
When you operate from overflow, you attract more overflow.
Abundance isn't just about money, it's a way of seeing the world.
It is waking up and feeling deep gratitude for the breath in your body.
It is feeling wealthy simply because you have access to the beauty of life.
It is looking at the trees, the sky, the sunrise—
and saying: I already have everything I need.

I know you're afraid.
I know you're wondering,
"What if it doesn't work?"
But sis, let me ask you something—
What if you fully surrendered?
What if you stopped trying to control every outcome and simply trusted the journey?
What if you stopped worrying about how it will happen and simply decided that it will?

Because here's the truth:

You were built for this.

Your success is inevitable.

The only thing you have to do is step into it.

Activation

Take a deep breath.

Now, say these words out loud:

I do not hustle. I align.

I am already wealthy in more ways than I can count.

Everything I desire is already on its way to me.

I surrender. I trust. I receive.

Let these words settle into your spirit.

Because your success is already written.

Reflection Questions

1. How does alignment feel in my body? What signs do I notice when something is right for me?
2. Where in my life have I been forcing instead of flowing?
3. What would happen if I truly trusted in divine timing?
4. Where am I still operating from a scarcity mindset? How can I shift into an abundance mindset?
5. If success was already guaranteed, how would I move differently?

Journal Space

Use this page to reflect on the questions—or write what your spirit needs to say.

_____

_____

_____

_____

_____

_____

_____

_____

_____

_____

_____

_____

_____

_____

_____

_____

Chapter 20: Becoming Limitless

For so long, I didn't realize I was trapped.
Not physically—
but mentally, emotionally, spiritually.
I was caught in cycles, reacting to life instead of shaping it.
But something inside of me always knew there was more.
Stepping into limitlessness isn't about doing more—
it's about *becoming* more.
It's about shifting your awareness so you stop fighting with life
and start flowing with it.
It's about realizing that time isn't linear, struggle isn't required,
and everything you desire already exists.
But first, you have to awaken to it.

The Nine Levels of Consciousness

Consciousness is not just a state, it is a spectrum.
A series of awakenings.
A process of expansion.
Every level brings you closer to your divine power, your universal
oneness, and your ability to create reality itself.

Here is the full breakdown of what this journey looked like for me:

1. Survival Mode – The State of Fight or Flight

This is where most people stay stuck.
Every decision is made in this state out of fear, scarcity, or
desperation.
Your nervous system is in a constant state of stress.
You react instead of responding.
Life feels like one crisis after another.

What it felt like: Everything was a struggle.

My body was tense, my mind was cluttered, and my spirit was restless. I was constantly worried about money, relationships, and my future.

I was living in survival, not truly living.

The shift: I realized that peace was even possible for me.

I didn't have to fight every battle, solve every problem, or carry every burden alone.

2. Self-Awareness – Recognizing the Patterns

When you move beyond survival, you start noticing things.

You start seeing yourself, your reactions, your choices.

You stop moving through life on autopilot.

What it felt like: I started questioning why I kept going back to situations that drained me.

I noticed how I responded to things, how I handled conflict, and how I coped with discomfort.

The shift: The moment I understood that my experiences weren't just happening to me—I was playing a role in them.

3. Self-Responsibility – Owning Your Power

This is the hardest shift for most people because it requires accountability.

It means recognizing that no one else is responsible for your happiness, your healing, your growth.

What it felt like: I stopped blaming others.

I stopped waiting for someone to save me.

I realized that my power had been in my hands the whole time.

The shift: The moment I stopped saying
"Why is this happening to me?" And started saying,
"What is this trying to teach me?"

4. Inner Healing – Transforming Pain into Wisdom
Once you take responsibility, you begin the real work—
healing the wounds that shaped you.
This is the level where you stop running from your emotions and
start sitting with them.

What it felt like: I finally faced the pain I had been avoiding for
years. I allowed myself to grieve, to feel, to release.

The shift: Realizing that healing isn't about erasing your past,
it's about integrating it, making peace with it and using it to build
something greater.

5. Expansion of Perception – Seeing Life Differently
This is when things start clicking.
You stop seeing the world as something happening to you.
You realize that everything is connected.
You see the patterns, the synchronicities, and the way energy
moves.

What it felt like: Life didn't feel random anymore.
I started noticing how my thoughts influenced my reality.
I saw the signs, the universal nudges, the ways my energy shaped
my experiences.

The shift: Understanding that reality is fluid.
Nothing is truly set in stone— except for what you believe to be
true.

6. Universal Connection – Feeling One with Everything

This is where separation dissolves.

You stop seeing yourself as a singular being and start feeling connected to everything.

The universe isn't just something outside of you—it is you.

What it felt like: Time started feeling different.
I didn't feel rushed—I didn't feel anxious.
I felt carried by something bigger than myself.
I trusted in a way I never had before.

The shift: The realization that I no longer needed to struggle for what was already mine.

7. Conscious Creation – Manifesting in Real Time

This is when you stop hoping and start knowing.

You don't wonder if things will happen—you know they already exist. The only thing left to do is align with them.

What it felt like: The things I once worked so hard for just started flowing to me. The money, the resources, the right people—they showed up naturally.

The shift: Understanding that manifestation isn't about forcing, it's about allowing.

8. Universal Flow – Living Without Resistance

At this level, you are in constant harmony with the universe.
You release the need to control or hold on.
You trust so fully that you no longer worry about outcomes.

What it felt like: Detachment and freedom.
A deep knowing that everything is unfolding perfectly.
Even when things didn't go as I planned, I didn't fight it—
I knew it was happening for me, not to me.

The shift: The moment I surrendered completely and allowed the universe to guide me.

9. Enlightenment – The State of Pure Being

This is the highest level of consciousness.
In this state, you don't strive—you simply are.
You no longer need to chase or prove.
You are fully present, anchored in peace, and aligned with your divine essence. Your presence radiates the harmony of the universe.

What it felt like: Stillness and presence.
A feeling of deep, unshakable peace, no matter what was happening around me.

The shift: The understanding that there is nothing left to become— I already am.

The Key to Flow and Freedom

Detachment is freedom.
Detachment doesn't mean you don't care.
It means you no longer cling.
It means you no longer push.

You no longer try to make people be who you want them to be—
You allow them to show you who they are.
You no longer rush things to happen on your timeline—
You trust that things will unfold in divine timing.

Activation

Sit in stillness.
Close your eyes.
Feel your energy settle.
Now, whisper to yourself:

I trust the flow of my life.
I am in alignment, not in pursuit.
What is meant for me cannot miss me.
I am free from struggle, free from fear, free from limitation.
I walk in my power, in my divinity, in my destiny.

Breathe.
Let go.
And step into your limitless self.

Reflection Questions

1. What level of consciousness do I feel most aligned with right now?
2. Where in my life am I still gripping instead of trusting?
3. What would change if I moved from resistance to ease?
4. What signs has the universe been sending me that I need to pay attention to?
5. How can I practice detachment in my relationships, goals, and daily life?

Journal Space

Use this page to reflect on the questions—or write what your spirit needs to say.

Chapter 21: Your Arrival

There is a moment in every awakened woman's journey when she knows, truly knows—
there is no going back.
She no longer questions her worth.
She no longer entertains illusions of limitation.
She no longer moves through life as if she is at the mercy of fate.
Because she remembers now.

She is the source.
She is the creator.
She is the universe in motion.
She is not waiting—
she is arriving.

The world moves differently around her now.
Doors open before she even reaches for the handle.
Opportunities fall into her lap, like whispers from the universe.
People feel her presence before she even speaks.
And she is simply being.

Because that's what an awakened woman does.
She trusts the pull, not the push.
She honors what flows and lets go of what resists.
Her power is in her release.
This is who you are now.

The Realization

The greatest lesson in all of this?
You were powerful all along.
They told you that you needed to outsource your power.

That you needed permission.
That you needed a blueprint, a title, external validation.
But the truth?
You create the energy.
You bend reality.
You are the alchemist.

Your power was never in someone choosing you.
Your power was never in someone seeing you.
Your power was never in proving your worth.
Your power was always in knowing that you were never lacking.

That you were never in competition.
That you were never missing anything.
You just had to remember.
And now you do.

Shifts in Energy, Mindset and Magnetism

You used to think life was happening to you.
But now you know —
life is happening *for* you.
You once saw obstacles, blocks, and resistance.
Now you understand:
your mind was the only thing in your way.
You believed in lack, limitation, and struggle until you
remembered your thoughts carry power.
And energy? It bends to your will.

That shift, that deep, unshakable knowing, it made you magnetic.
You don't fear the unknown. You surrender to it.
You don't seek validation. You radiate self-certainty.
You don't explain. You embody.

You move with intention.
You flow with confidence.
You rise with resilience.
You meet life with ease—
not because it's always easy, but because you no longer resist
what's meant for you.
And nothing—
not doubt, not fear, not anyone's expectations can shake you.

You are anchored now.

Activation

Tonight, I want you to stand in front of the mirror.
Look into your own eyes. Witness the woman who has emerged.
Place your hand over your heart. Feel your power.
Speak these words aloud:

I am the embodiment of certainty.
I am the woman I once prayed to become.
I trust. I surrender. I align.
I am powerful beyond measure.

Then, I invite you to play *"Ascension (Rebirth)"* by King Sis.
Sing it to yourself—
not just as a song, but as a vow.
When she sings:

"I just want to make me yours, I just want to make you mine,"
sing it *to yourself.*

As if you are proposing to your own soul.

Place your hand over your heart.
If you're playing it through a speaker, touch the speaker with your
other hand.
Feel the vibration move through you.
Experience the frequency —
not just the sound.

Let it sink into your cells.
Let it reprogram you.
Let it awaken what's been dormant.

I do this often —
allowing the music to carry me into a higher frequency.
A rebirth.
And every time, I feel the shift.
The tears come —
not from sadness, but from the overwhelming love I feel for
myself in that moment.
A soul-deep knowing that I am witnessing my own rebirth —
over and over again.
And no, I don't want to lose this high.

Now, take one deep breath in.
As you exhale, feel everything that is not you dissolve.
Feel the shift.
Feel the completion.
This is not just who you are *becoming*.
This is who you already are.
And the universe is responding.

Reflection Questions

1. What is the most profound realization I've had about myself on this journey?
2. If I could sit with my past self, what would I whisper to her?
3. How has my energy shifted? How does the world respond to me now?
4. Where do I still feel resistance? What is keeping me from fully stepping into my power?

Journal Space

Use this page to reflect on the questions—or write what your spirit needs to say.

_____

_____

_____

_____

_____

_____

_____

_____

_____

_____

_____

_____

_____

_____

_____

_____

_____

_____

Sanctuary Within *(Interlude)*

Inspired by *"Do It Well"* by *dvsn*

There was a moment—
one that lives in my body more than in words.
When I listened to this song not as if someone else was singing it
to me, but as if I was singing it to myself.
And then it hit me.

"And you're the only therapy I know…"

I placed my hand on my heart, looked at myself in the mirror, and
let those words land in my body like a vow.

Because I am.

I am my own therapy.
I am the safest place I've ever known.
Not because life has always been gentle with me.
But because I have made myself gentle.
I have cultivated stillness.
I have chosen softness.
I have learned to mother my pain—
to honor my wounds and to wrap my arms around every version of
me that ever thought she wasn't enough.
That's what makes me the safest place to land.
And I want this for you, too.
Not a perfect version of you.
Not a version that never gets triggered or tired.
But a version that knows how to return home to herself.
A version that sings love songs to herself.
That breathes into her body like a prayer.
That holds her heart like the sacred thing it is.

You are the only therapy you've ever truly needed.
Everything else is a tool to help you remember that.

Activation

Find a quiet space. Dim the lights.
Play *"Do It Well"* by *dvsn* and stand in front of your mirror.
Place one hand over your heart.
Gaze at yourself—really see her.
And when the lyric comes,

"And you're the only therapy I know…"

Sing it to yourself. Let the words echo in your body.
Let the vibration of the music move through your soul.
Let your presence become the sanctuary you return to.
Breathe into that moment, receive it.
Let the tears come if they do.
Let the knowing land.

You are home.

Reflection Questions

1. What does it feel like in my body when I am the safest place I know?
2. How do I respond to myself when I am hurting, unseen, or afraid?
3. Where in my life have I withheld softness from myself and how can I offer it now?
4. If I sang a love song to the parts of me I've abandoned— what would I say?

Journal Space

Use this page to reflect on the questions—or write what your spirit needs to say.

_____

_____

_____

_____

_____

_____

_____

_____

_____

_____

_____

_____

_____

_____

_____

_____

_____

_____

_____

_____

_____

Chapter 22: Your Sacred Contract

There comes a moment at the end of every initiation.
A threshold, a choice.
This is *that* moment.
You have walked through fire.
You have burned down the versions of yourself that were never truly yours.
You have unlearned, unraveled, and reclaimed yourself, piece by piece.
You are not the same woman who began this journey.
But before you close this chapter, there is one last thing you must do.
You must swear an oath to yourself.
Not just any promise—
a sacred contract.
This is the moment where you claim yourself, fully.
Where you vow, without hesitation, that you will never again abandon the woman you have become.

Say it out loud, write it down.
Commit to yourself the way you once begged others to commit to you.
This is the moment where you choose yourself, forever.

The Oath

I swear to love you fiercely.

I swear to never again negotiate your worth.

I swear to never keep you prisoner in spaces that diminish your light.

I swear to never ignore you when you are in need.

I swear to accept every part of you and never suppress how you feel again.

I swear to worship you like the goddess you've always been.

I swear to look at you, touch you, nourish you in a way that makes it impossible for anyone to ever feed you crumbs again.

I swear to give you the love you deserve—
first, fully, and always—
before seeking it from anyone else.

And you will never again abandon yourself for the comfort of others.

Final Words

Before you move on, I want you to sit with something:
How did it feel in your body when you spoke those words over yourself?
When you promised yourself those things?
Where did you feel it?
Did your chest tighten?
Did your heart expand?
Did your body soften or resist?

And if nothing came up at all—
I want you to ask yourself why.
Why would you get all the way to this part of your journey—
through all the shedding, through all the burning, through all the rising, and still hesitate to have that kind of reverence for yourself?

Why would you hold back from making the one promise that
matters most—
to never abandon yourself again?
To never go back to the very thing that brought you to your knees?

Sit with it.
Breathe through it.

Because this is not just about finishing a book.
This is about deciding who you will be from this moment forward.

The Benediction

I need you to know something before you close this book:
I didn't write this from a place of theory.
I wasn't sitting in some cozy corner imagining what healing *might*
feel like.
I lived through every page with you.
Some parts I had already mastered —
like my emotions, like surrender.
But there were other parts I was still wrestling with even as I wrote
them down.
Especially when it came to permission—
permission to experience pleasure, to talk about sensuality, to be
honest about self-pleasure without shame.
There was a moment when I almost took those parts out.
I thought maybe they were too bold.
Too much.
Maybe I should soften it, keep it safer, make it easier for people to
digest.
But then I heard that inner voice—
my higher self—saying:
Put it back.
It belongs.
This is exactly why you have to say it.
Because if even I hesitated to talk about my own pleasure,
then I knew there were other women who needed permission too.
So I left it in here.
And I'm glad I did.
Because you deserve a guide that wasn't written from distance.
You deserve a guide that was *lived*.

There are plenty of books out there written from theory.
Plenty of words that sound beautiful but don't actually touch the
real places inside you.

That's not what this was ever meant to be.
This was a walk through the fire with you.
This was a hand on your back saying: *Keep going*.
This was me, standing right beside you, every step you chose to take closer to yourself.
And now that you're standing here—
you get to choose how you move forward.

And I know you know this by now,
But allow me to remind you:
The work doesn't stop here.
There is no finish line to healing.
Only deeper layers.
Deeper remembrance.
There will be moments you think you've arrived, and then life will invite you even deeper.
There will be days when you feel fully whole, and then something will crack you open again.
It's not failure.
It's expansion.
You're not broken.
You're becoming.

And when those moments come—
and they will, I want you to remember this:
You are not starting over.
You are meeting a new version of yourself who deserves the same love, the same grace, the same protection you promised her back at the beginning of this journey.
If you need to, come back to these pages.
Come back and remember how far you've already come.
Come back and remember the woman you chose to become.
You're not walking alone.

I'm still right beside you—
hand in hand, whispering in your ear:

Keep going.
Keep choosing yourself.
Keep trusting your own light.

You are the miracle.
You are the answered prayer.

And if this book felt like a return—
then the next one will feel like a reckoning.
Because once you awaken,
you'll have to *guard* what you've remembered.
You'll have to *live it out loud* —
even when the world tries to pull you back asleep.

In my next offering, I will walk with you through that too.
We're just getting started.

With all my heart,

Tacara

A Glimpse of What's Next...

The journey doesn't end here.
The Gospel is where the reckoning happens.
It's where we go deeper.
It's where we confront the roots, not just the branches.
Because what you've lived through—
the shrinking, the silencing, the self-abandonment, didn't just start
with the family dysfunction we unpacked during your awakening.
It wasn't just the misaligned relationships.
It wasn't just the men, missed opportunities, or the hard seasons.
It started long before you ever took your first breath.
It started when they made our grandmothers forget who the hell
they were.
It started when they taught them to shrink inside their roles, to be
silent inside their homes, to outsource their power to pulpits and
instead of their own inner knowing.

And we, without even realizing it, inherited that silence.
We inherited that shrinking.
We learned to show up small because that's what we saw.
We learned to abandon ourselves because they had to survive by
doing the same.

The Gospel is about reclaiming what they were forced to forget.
It's about remembering the power that lives in your bloodline—
and choosing to carry it forward healed, whole, and sovereign.
It's about refusing to live one more generation under the weight of
what was never yours to carry.

Excerpt from *The Gospel*

You were taught that 10% was the seed.
But what if the real breakthrough came when you started pouring
that same 10% back into you?
Not into a basket.
Not into a pastor's vacation fund.
Not into a building project.
But into your healing. Your growth. Your freedom.
They've got people believing that the currency of heaven is
money —
when really, it's devotion to self.
To knowing yourself. To owning yourself.
To discerning the lies from the truth.
To rebuilding belief in your own divine instruction.
The real product of the church is not transformation.
It's the next feel-good message.
They pass it out every Sunday and maybe again on Wednesday if
you're really devoted.
A little hope. A little guilt.
And if you're lucky? You might walk out of there feeling
worthy —
for a few hours.
But they don't teach you how to build.
They don't teach you how to discern.
They don't teach you how to own your yes or your no.
They teach you how to give.

But imagine if instead of dropping that 10% into a basket every
week, you dropped it into:

- A savings account
- A Roth IRA
- A therapist's office
- A coach who holds you accountable

- A writing workshop
- A business course
- A vision board
- A deep rest day
- A massage
- A passport renewal
- A healing retreat

You know what you have after that?
A foundation.

Back in Chapter 3, when I first taught you how to begin doing
shadow work, I told you this work would require curiosity.
I told you that you had to be willing to chase the fire—
not fear getting burned by it.
This is the fire I was talking about.
This is the fire I was preparing you for.

As I walked you through your awakening, parts of it were raw.
Unapologetic. Heavy.
But now we're going deeper.
Now, we're going to the roots.
And it's going to feel different.
It'll make you question everything you were ever taught.
But if you had the courage to peel back the layers of your own
awakening, then it shouldn't scare you, and it sure shouldn't
offend you to go here with me.

So meet me there.